All rights reserved.
Copyright © 2023 Sandhya Jane

The book "200+ Inspirational Quotes for Everyday Life and Work" is intended for personal use only. It is not permitted to reproduce, resell, or share this book with others. To share with someone else, please purchase an official copy. If you are reading this without owning the book or obtaining it through official channels, kindly contact the author (sandhya@sandhyajane.com or Sandhya.jane@gmail.com) to acquire an official copy.

Thank you for respecting the author's hard work and the effort put in by the organization to create this content. This initial version is a test draft and will be continually improved in terms of quality, presentation, citations, and more in the future.

Permission is necessary for any reuse or distribution of this book.

Copyright © 2023
Sandhya Jane

200+ Inspirational
Quotes for Everyday Life
and Work

Inspirational Quote Book

Living in today's fast-paced, constantly evolving, and increasingly challenging world emphasizes the importance of seeking inspiration and motivation in our daily lives. One effective method is starting and ending the day with a positive quote, setting the right tone for each day.

Reading from this book in the morning can influence the day ahead, while reading it at night can help in planning for the following day, year, and life in general. These quotes offer valuable insights that serve as reminders of the strength of positivity and resilience.

The inspirational quote book acts as a valuable collection of guidance and wisdom, capable of uplifting and inspiring readers from all backgrounds. Inspirational thoughts have the power to rewire our minds, encouraging us to keep moving forward through both challenging and joyful times.

Investing time and money into reading inspirational quote books proves to be highly beneficial for personal growth and development.

This book presents wise and practical quotes to guide everyday life and work.

Bhagmad Gita says,
"Watch your thoughts, for they transform into words.
" Watch your words, for they turn into actions.
"Watch your actions, for they become habits.
"Watch your habits, for they become your character."
"Finally, it's your character that shapes your life.

Hence, setting the tone or focus through practical and meaningful quotes is recommended every day.

I truly hope this book brings positivity and changes your life eventually...

Inspirational quotes offer a wealth of wisdom that transcends time and place, providing a valuable source of motivation and insight. By reading them, we gain access to the collective experiences and wisdom of others, allowing us to learn lessons that we may not encounter in our own lives. These quotes act as bite-sized nuggets of inspiration, offering valuable insights into life's challenges and triumphs.

One of the primary benefits of reading inspirational quotes is the opportunity to understand the multifaceted messages behind them. Many quotes have multiple layers of meaning that can be unpacked and explored through deeper reflection. This process allows readers to connect with the wisdom embedded in these quotes and see how others have navigated obstacles.

Furthermore, reading inspirational quotes encourages self-reflection. As we correlate the messages with our own thoughts and values, we gain a deeper understanding of ourselves.

This self-reflection process fosters personal growth, helping us to become more resilient and insightful individuals. In essence, inspirational quotes provide a bridge to greater self-awareness and personal development.

-- Sandhya Jane

My grandmother, the late Mrs. Nilamma Jane, conveyed her wisdom through her daily deeds, devoting her life to resilience, survival, assistance, and motivation.

Adhering to Hindu customs, she followed Dinacharya and Ritucharya, observing Hindu festivals and rituals with great dedication.

Every morning, she would prepare three rotis for the cow, crow, and dog before cooking for the family and Swamiji.

Her actions instilled in us the importance of traditional practices, generosity, and empathy in our everyday routines.

"SOHAM"
I AM THAT I AM

EVERYTHING
IS
WITHIN ME

SANDHYA JANE
AUTHOR
@Sandhyajane.com

Sandhya Jane

> **"**
>
> Simplify and focus on your life; you'll achieve more than you realize.
>
> **"**
>
> **SANDHYA JANE**
> AUTHOR

@Sandhyajane.com

Sandhya Jane

> **99**
>
> Focus and focus and focus - it's the only way to build a successful life.
>
> **99**
>
> SANDHYA JANE
> AUTHOR

@Sandhyajane.com

Sandhya Jane

> Life is useless if you cannot do anything for others.

SANDHYA JANE
AUTHOR & SPEAKER

@Sandhyajane.com

Sandhya Jane

> The first step is as significant as switching on the burner and bringing the water to boil before making pasta.
>
> **SANDHYA JANE**
> AUTHOR

@Sandhyajane.com

Sandhya Jane

> If you are afraid of doing anything, watch babies to learn how to be fearless of trying anything new.

SANDHYA JANE
AUTHOR

@Sandhyajane.com

Sandhya Jane

> **99**
> Manage, manipulate, or motivate; a true leader knows the difference between these three, and uses them effectively.
> **99**
>
> **SANDHYA JANE**
> AUTHOR

@Sandhyajane.com

Sandhya Jane

> CAN or CANNOT do it is a part of our thinking, it has nothing to do with our capability or capacity.

SANDHYA JANE
AUTHOR

@Sandhyajane.com

Sandhya Jane

> To instill the value of karma (work) and dharma (responsibilities) in a child, teach him the Ramayan and Mahabharat. Additionally, involve them in daily activities such as taking care of younger siblings, grandparents, pets, cleaning and cooking.

SANDHYA JANE
AUTHOR

@Sandhyajane.com

Sandhya Jane

> **99**
>
> Learning and acting on your learning is the only way to improve your life.
>
> **99**

SANDHYA JANE
AUTHOR

@Sandhyajane.com

Sandhya Jane

> Love your job; having a job is better than looking for one.

SANDHYA JANE
AUTHOR

@Sandhyajane.com

Sandhya Jane

> ❝
>
> Discipline yourself to complete your tasks on time; tasks become assignments, assignments become projects, projects build portfolios, and portfolios build a career...
>
> ❞
>
> **SANDHYA JANE**
> AUTHOR

@Sandhyajane.com

Artificial Intelligence

The Internet made us borderless, AI has potential to make us faceless. It means there is a risk of creative or scientific work with AI being duplicated by remaining faceless, irresponsible, and unaccountable.

SANDHYA JANE

AUTHOR

@Sandhyajane.com

Sandhya Jane

> I can't do it? Well, you CAN do it. Just list your reasons and overcome them one by one.

SANDHYA JANE
AUTHOR

@Sandhyajane.com

Artificial Intelligenc[e]

Creativity is a major factor in AI. How you conceptualize and deploy AI technology will make all the difference in your business or professional life.

SANDHYA JANE
AUTHOR
— 99 —
@Sandhyajane.com

Sandhya Jane

> ""
>
> If you want to choose between character and experience, choose the person with character because experience can always be added later.
>
> ""
>
> **SANDHYA JANE**
> AUTHOR

@Sandhyajane.com

Sandhya Jane

> **99**
>
> Every relationship is beyond the concept of 50-50 equality as everyone in the relationship has a role to play and every role has its own significance that is beyond comparison.
>
> **99**
>
> **SANDHYA JANE**
> AUTHOR

@Sandhyajane.com

Sandhya Jane

> Dincharya: A disciplined and well-organized daily life will lead to an accomplished life.

SANDHYA JANE
AUTHOR
@Sandhyajane.com

Sandhya Jane

— 99 —

Focus on your goals and work hard to achieve them. It will produce either an achievement or an experience.

— 99 —

SANDHYA JANE
AUTHOR

@Sandhyajane.com

Sandhya Jane

> "
> CAN and CANNOT do it is a part of our thinking; it has nothing to do with our capability or capacity.
> "

SANDHYA JANE
AUTHOR

@Sandhyajane.com

Sandhya Jane

> Connecting and collaborating means empowering and enriching everyone involved in the process...

SANDHYA JANE
AUTHOR

@Sandhyajane.com

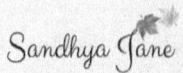

>
>
> Shri Ram faced many hurdles and temptations during his lifetime; however, he chose to remain faithful to his values. That is his character. For this, billions of people continue to worship Bhagwan Shri Ram thousands of years later.
>
> **SANDHYA JANE**
> AUTHOR

@Sandhyajane.com

Sandhya Jane

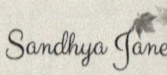

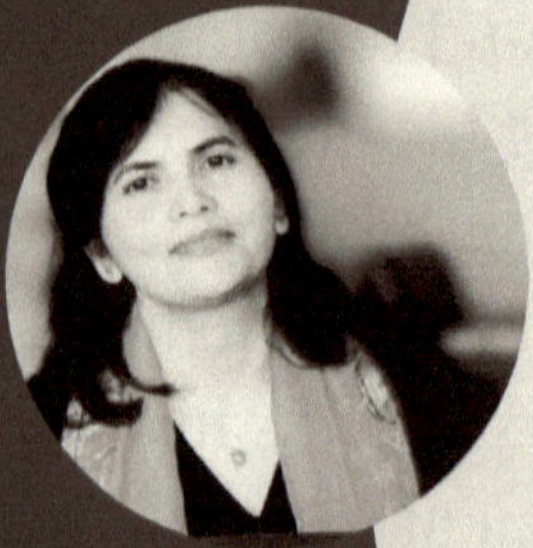

A sound strategy is like a chase board: before making a decision, think about all the risks and rewards.

SANDHYA JANE
AUTHOR

@Sandhyajane.com

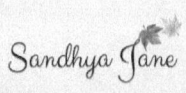

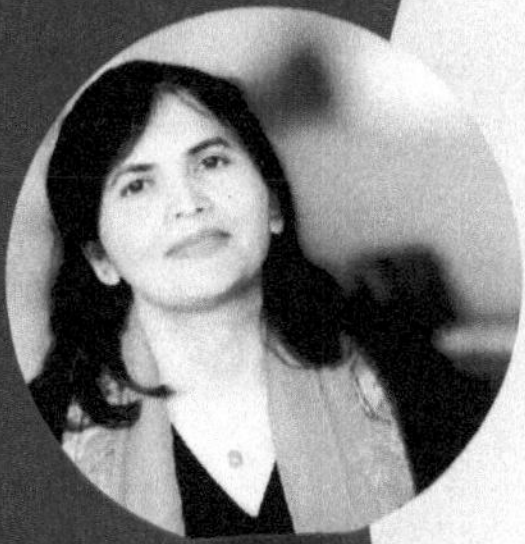

> Investments in your time learning or supporting others cannot be substituted.

SANDHYA JANE
AUTHOR

@Sandhyajane.com

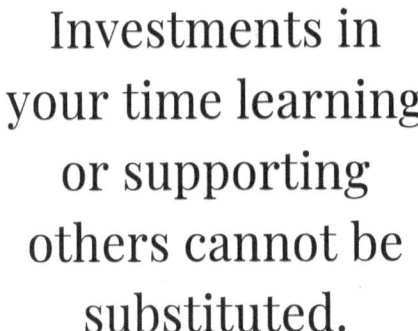

Sandhya Jane

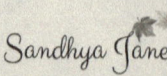

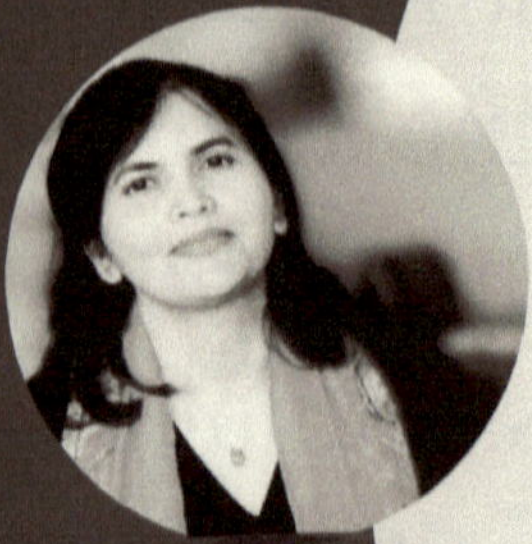

A person traveling to different countries and networking with scholars increases his intellect in the same way as a drop of oil spreads in water.

SANDHYA JANE
AUTHOR

@Sandhyajane.com

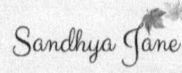

> Dincharya: The power of routine is often underestimated in creating a successful life; it takes away daily disturbances and lets you focus on daily priorities.

SANDHYA JANE
AUTHOR

@Sandhyajane.com

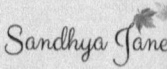

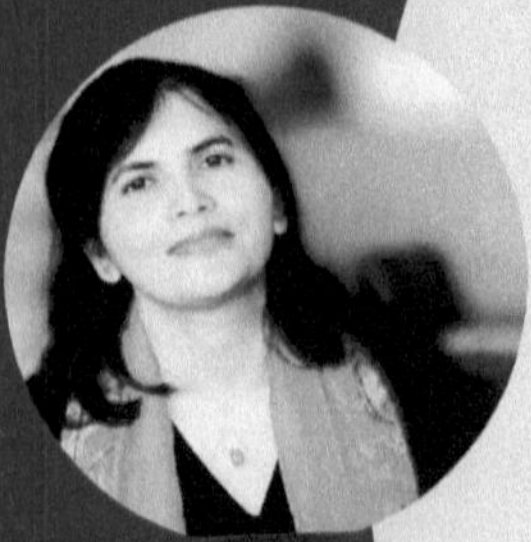

> When someone is drowning, he needs a help to get out, not a philosophy; everything has its own significance at the right time. Mentoring and handholding are critical for creating future leaders.

SANDHYA JANE
AUTHOR

@Sandhyajane.com

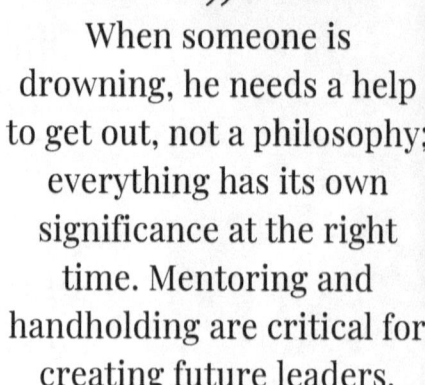

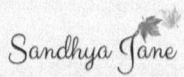

> Doers are always winners... a million-dollar idea in realization is better than a trillion-dollar idea in the head.

SANDHYA JANE
AUTHOR

@Sandhyajane.com

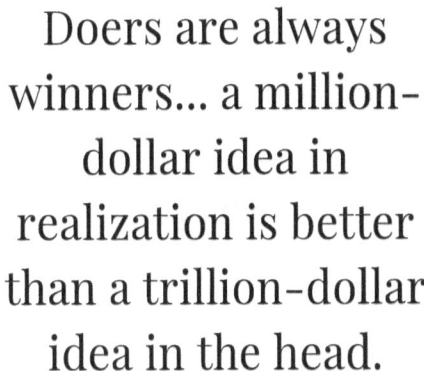

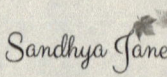

Sandhya Jane

Learning new skills and excelling at them accelerates your growth.

SANDHYA JANE

AUTHOR

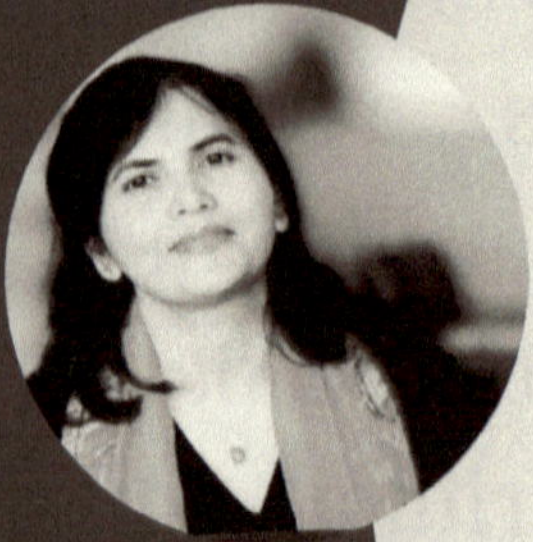

@Sandhyajane.com

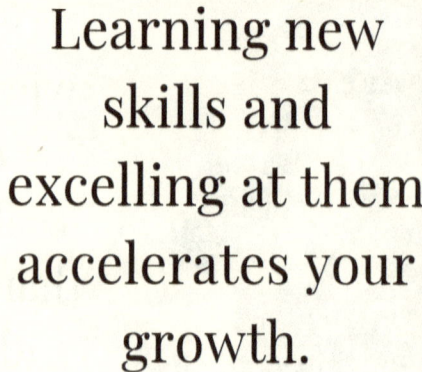

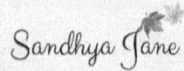

> **Probability of failure is 100% if you don't take the first step...**

SANDHYA JANE
AUTHOR

@Sandhyajane.com

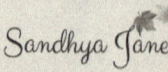

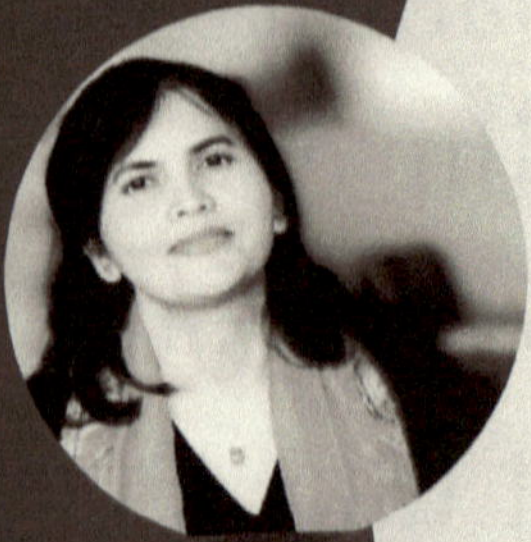

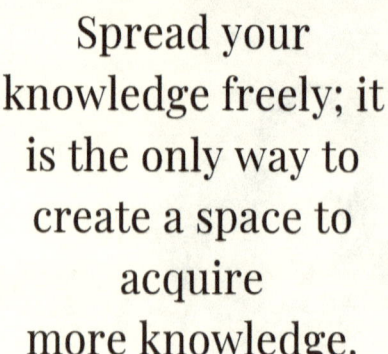

> Spread your knowledge freely; it is the only way to create a space to acquire more knowledge.

SANDHYA JANE
AUTHOR

@Sandhyajane.com

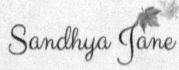

> Once you end a project and list your lessons learned, don't reassess over and over again; instead, focus your energy and experience on your next project.

SANDHYA JANE
AUTHOR

@Sandhyajane.com

Sandhya Jane

> **"What am I in others' eyes"** is not significant; but, **"What am I in my eyes"** is the most important...

SANDHYA JANE
AUTHOR

@Sandhyajane.com

Sandhya Jane

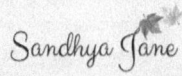

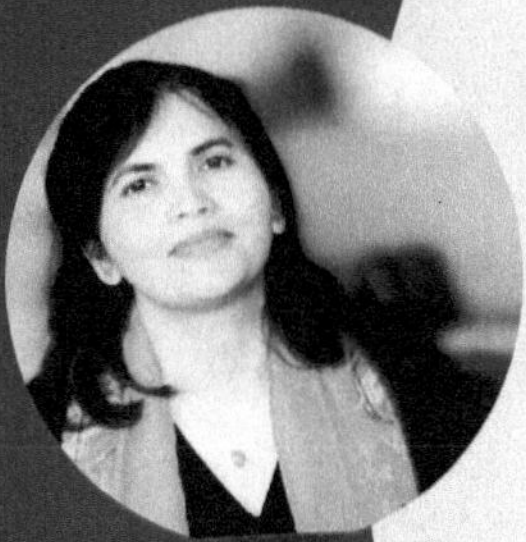

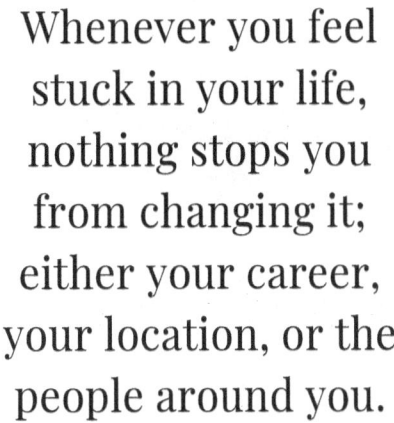

Whenever you feel stuck in your life, nothing stops you from changing it; either your career, your location, or the people around you.

SANDHYA JANE

AUTHOR

@Sandhyajane.com

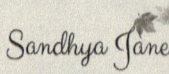

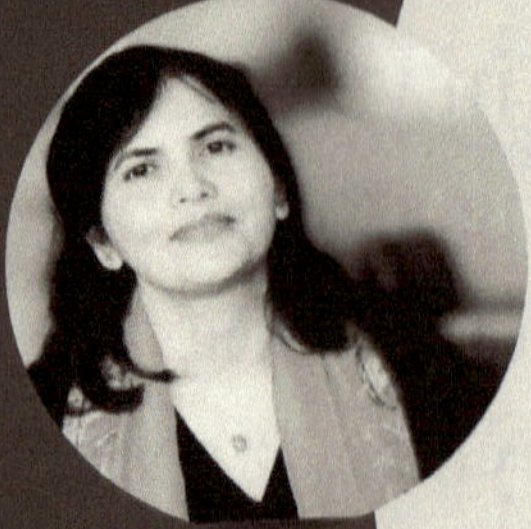

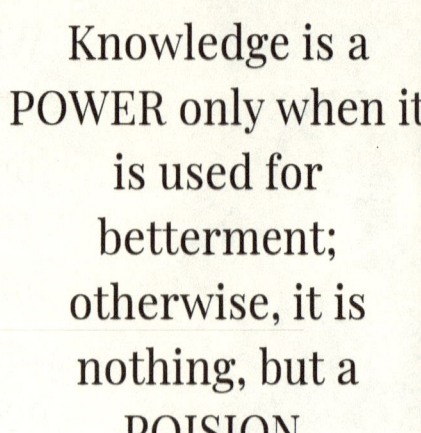

> **"**
>
> Knowledge is a POWER only when it is used for betterment; otherwise, it is nothing, but a POISION.
>
> **"**
>
> **SANDHYA JANE**
> AUTHOR

@Sandhyajane.com

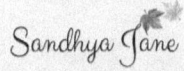

> The only way to build a successful career is through continuous improvement in your knowledge and skills. This is even more needed when you reach the pinnacle as staying there is not easy.

SANDHYA JANE
AUTHOR

@Sandhyajane.com

Sandhya Jane

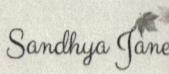

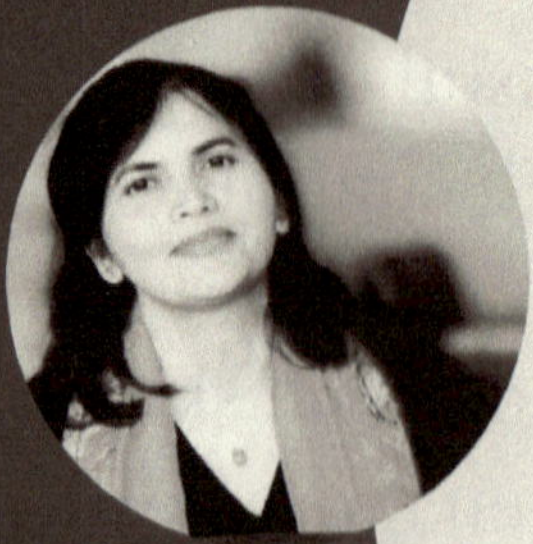

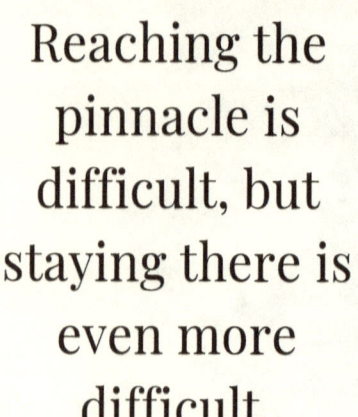

Reaching the pinnacle is difficult, but staying there is even more difficult.

SANDHYA JANE
AUTHOR

@Sandhyajane.com

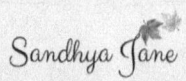

Sandhya Jane

> People who change their stand are dynamic, but people whose words/commitments remain unchanged are honorable.

SANDHYA JANE
AUTHOR

@Sandhyajane.com

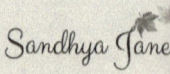

Sandhya Jane

You need a very little money to live happily; but you need lots of money to show others that you are living happily.

SANDHYA JANE
AUTHOR

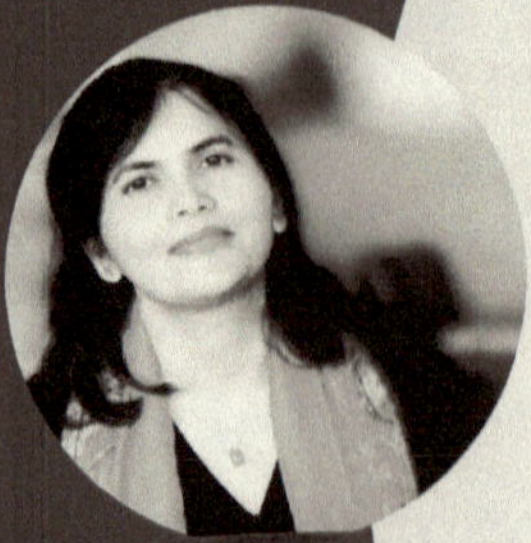

@Sandhyajane.com

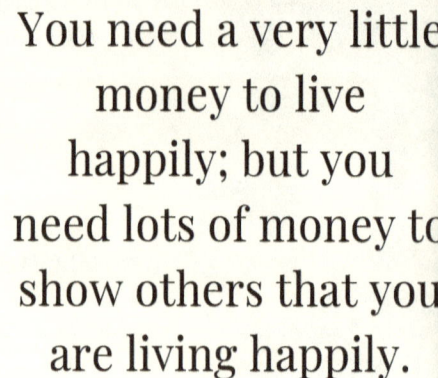

> The tree reveals its true color in winter; otherwise, every tree is green in spring.
>
> A relationship reveals its true color when you are facing adversity.

SANDHYA JANE
AUTHOR

@Sandhyajane.com

Sandhya Jane

> Urmila, wife of Shri Laxman (Bhagwan Shri Ram's younger brother) chose to sleep for 14 years for herself and her husband. She made a deal with goddess Nidra Devi (goddess of sleep) for this because she knew her husband had to remain awake to protect his brother (Shri Ram) and sister-in-law (Ma Sita). This shows how responsibilities are understood and shared them collectively in Hindu culture.

SANDHYA JANE
AUTHOR

@Sandhyajane.com

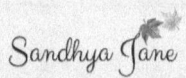

> **99**

Your virtuous thoughts/intentions cannot be killed by any poison, but malicious thoughts/intentions can kill any nectar.

99

SANDHYA JANE
AUTHOR

@Sandhyajane.com

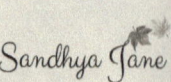

Sandhya Jane

> **"**
>
> You can live happily when you don't expect anything from others and others too don't expect anything from you; but that is not the meaning of life.
>
> **"**
>
> **SANDHYA JANE**
> AUTHOR

@Sandhyajane.com

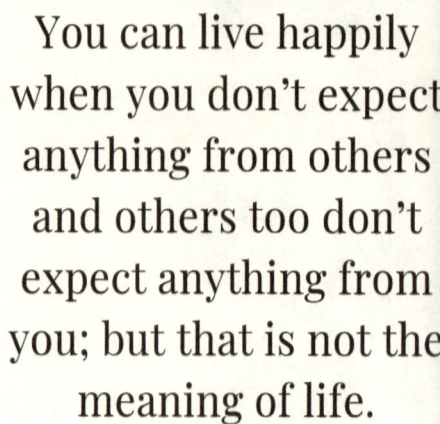

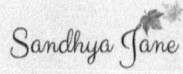

>
>
> The moon is a lamp in the evening, the sun is a lamp in the morning, Dharm is the lamp in the three worlds and the child is the lamp of the clan.
>
> **SANDHYA JANE**
> AUTHOR

@Sandhyajane.com

Sandhya Jane

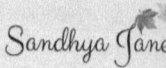

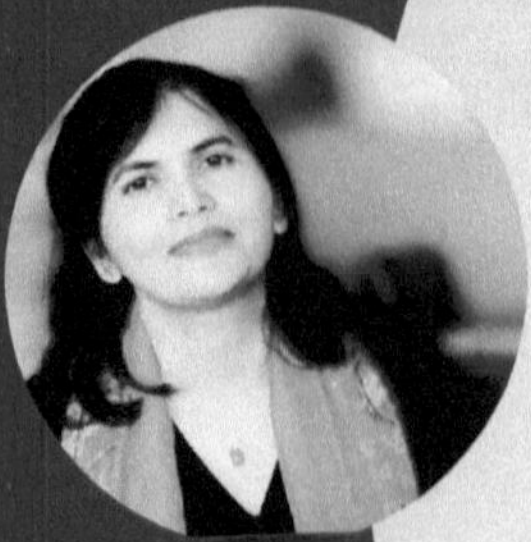

Bring elders and young people together. They bond well and inspire each other. One of the reasons the joint-family system works well in India and other Asian societies.

SANDHYA JANE

AUTHOR

@Sandhyajane.com

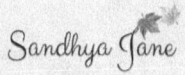

Sandhya Jane

> "
>
> We need to develop trust and understanding before building a relationship...
>
> "
>
> **SANDHYA JANE**
> AUTHOR

@Sandhyajane.com

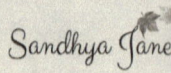

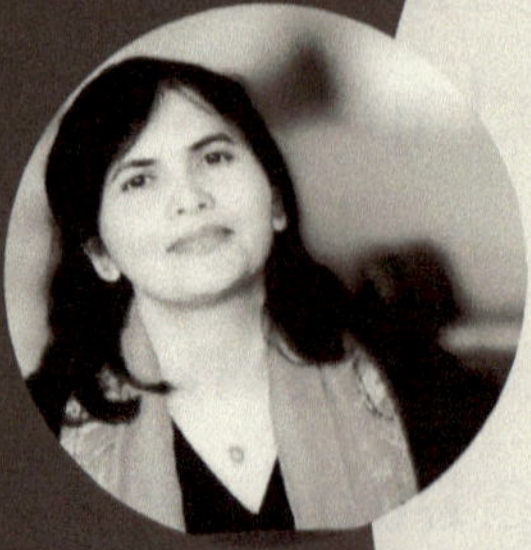

> **"**
>
> Who says you CANNOT? Except for you, nothing will matter between CAN and CANNOT.
>
> **"**
>
> **SANDHYA JANE**
> AUTHOR

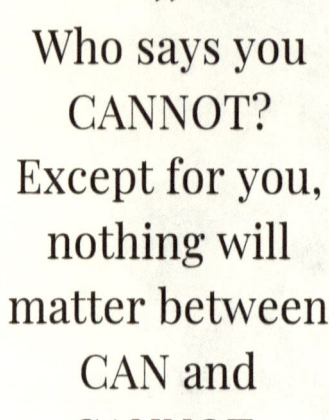

@Sandhyajane.com

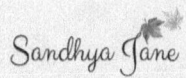

> Respect:
> When a powerful person forgives or a poor person donates, they become worthy of respect.

SANDHYA JANE
AUTHOR

@Sandhyajane.com

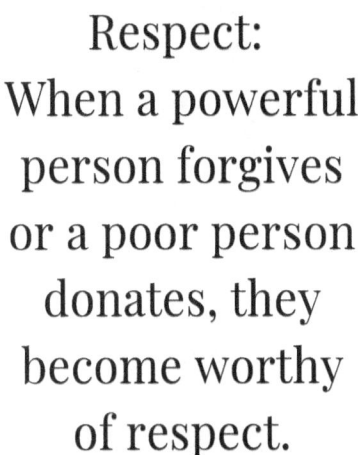

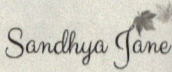

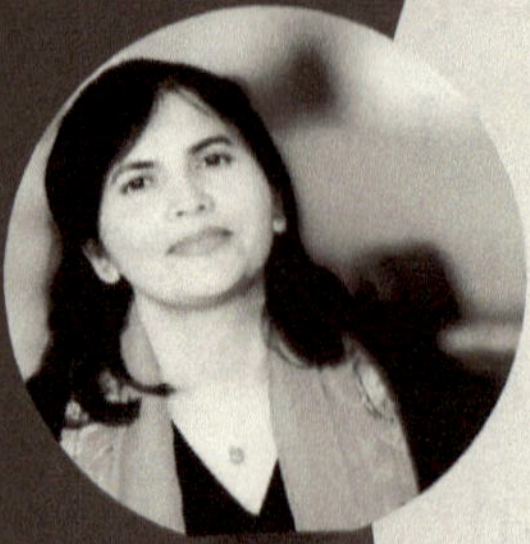

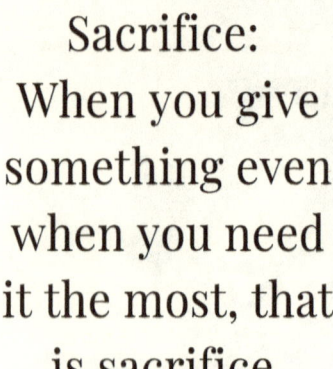

> **"**
>
> Sacrifice:
> When you give something even when you need it the most, that is sacrifice.
>
> **"**
>
> **SANDHYA JANE**
> AUTHOR

@Sandhyajane.com

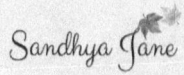

> ## Rich:
> If a hungry person donates food or a homeless individual takes in a stranger, he is richer than someone living in a 10 million dollar mansion.
>
> **SANDHYA JANE**
> AUTHOR

@Sandhyajane.com

Sandhya Jane

> **Bond:**
> Mother giving her meal to child or father giving his last earning to fulfill child's needs, are some of the examples of how strong family bonds are created in the world...

SANDHYA JANE
AUTHOR

@Sandhyajane.com

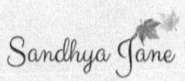

> **99**
>
> Willpower:
> If you lose something precious, don't worry; you can always get something better if you have willpower. Nothing is more precious than your willpower.
>
> **99**
>
> **SANDHYA JANE**
> AUTHOR

@Sandhyajane.com

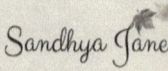
Sandhya Jane

> **"**
>
> Dealing with pain: The most effective way to heal a painful experience is to help others suffering from similar pain, and bring them out of it.
>
> **"**
>
> **SANDHYA JANE**
> AUTHOR

@Sandhyajane.com

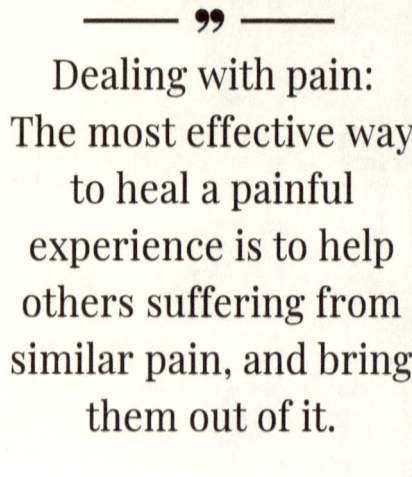

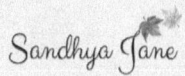

> **"**
>
> It is harmful if you do not speak truth or speak pleasantly; a truth spoken in a harsh manner and a lie told in a sweet manner, both are equally harmful.
>
> **"**
>
> **SANDHYA JANE**
> AUTHOR

@Sandhyajane.com

Sandhya Jane

> **Ignorance:**
> Ignorance is bliss, but not always. Consult mothers of infants, commandos, pilots, surgeons, etc., who are responsible for safeguarding others' lives.

SANDHYA JANE
AUTHOR

@Sandhyajane.com

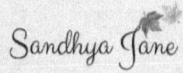

> Welcome the difficulties in life; they awaken your potential strength...

SANDHYA JANE
AUTHOR

@Sandhyajane.com

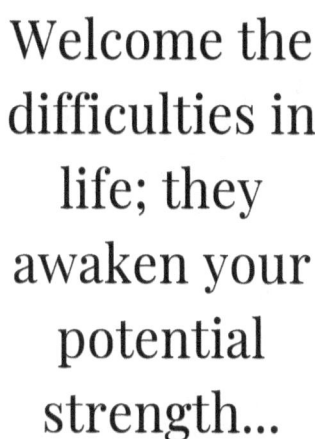

Sandhya Jane

> **99**
>
> If you are uncertain about something, breakdown the idea or problem and try to find out where it came from. Find out who will be affected, how they will be affected, etc. With these answers, you will automatically come up with possible solutions.
>
> **99**
>
> **SANDHYA JANE**
> AUTHOR

@Sandhyajane.com

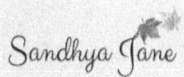

> If something is not working, try to work it out without stretching it too much; remember, there is a much larger life outside that crisis or goal or relationship or moment...

SANDHYA JANE
AUTHOR

@Sandhyajane.com

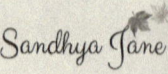

> 99
>
> Why my life is not perfect; hello, nobody's life is perfect, we have to prioritize 'what we want', and defocus on 'what we do not want'. Once we know, we need to shift the entire focus on 'what we want' and progress further. If you continue to work on them, you will eventually become better at them, which is one step towards mastering your field.
>
> 99
>
> **SANDHYA JANE**
> AUTHOR

@Sandhyajane.com

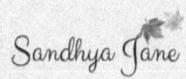

Sandhya Jane

> **Create a daily routine like a boss and follow it like a slave.**

SANDHYA JANE
AUTHOR

@Sandhyajane.com

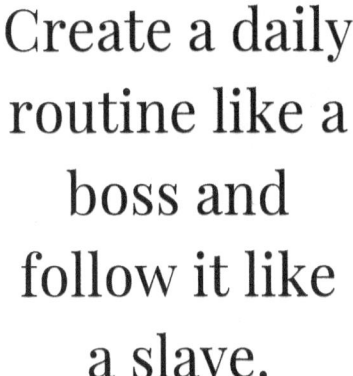

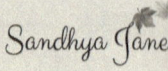

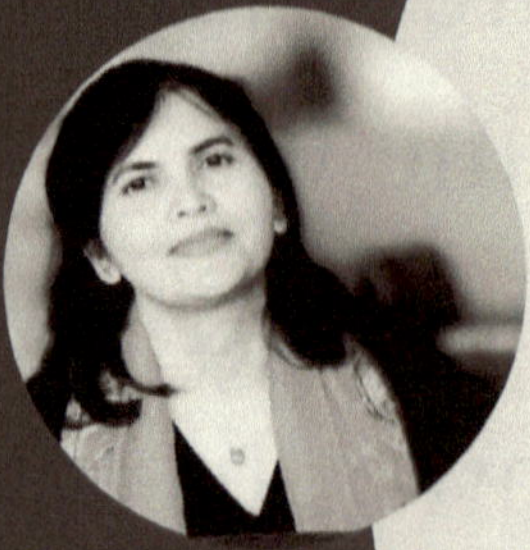

> **"**
> Forgiveness doesn't change the past, but the future gets better.
> **"**

SANDHYA JANE
AUTHOR

@Sandhyajane.com

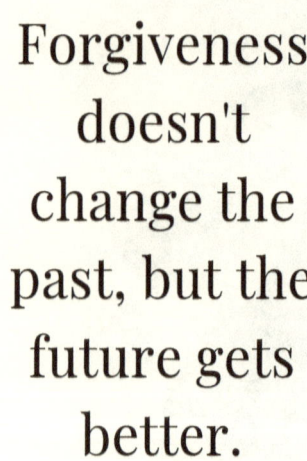

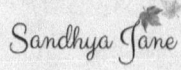

Sandhya Jane

> **"**
>
> When you reach a 'go' or 'no-go' state, simply list the benefits of doing it and the costs of not doing it. You will find the answers.
>
> **"**
>
> **SANDHYA JANE**
> AUTHOR

@Sandhyajane.com

Sandhya Jane

> "
>
> Experience and mistakes are inversely proportional; the more experience, the fewer mistakes.
>
> "

SANDHYA JANE
AUTHOR

@Sandhyajane.com

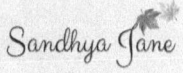

> **"**
>
> Business and personal losses are part of life; the more we detach ourselves from them, the better prepared we are to focus on future success.
>
> **"**
>
> **SANDHYA JANE**
> AUTHOR

@Sandhyajane.com

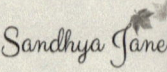

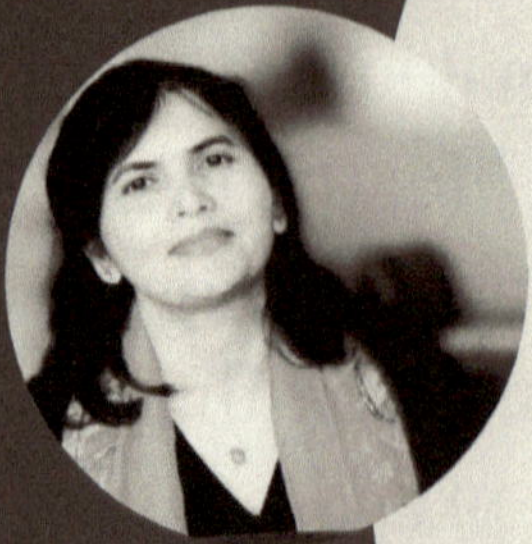

> If anyone rejects you, never go back to that person. Instead, value others in your life and focus on yourself to build a successful life.

SANDHYA JANE
AUTHOR

@Sandhyajane.com

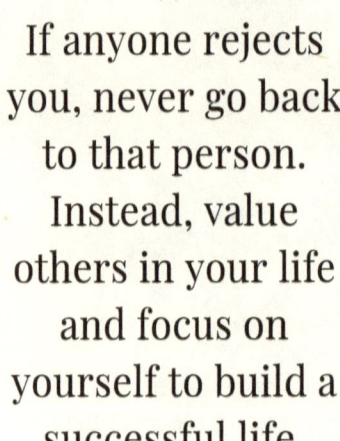

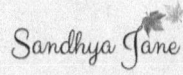

> **"**
>
> The day you feel you are an useless, list down all your good qualities that have helped you or others. See if any of them can be used again to help yourself or others.
>
> **"**
>
> **SANDHYA JANE**
> AUTHOR

@Sandhyajane.com

Sandhya Jane

> **Only love is not enough. It must be coupled with understanding and trust to last in any relationship.**

SANDHYA JANE
AUTHOR

@Sandhyajane.com

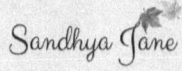
Sandhya Jane

> **99**
>
> Only your friends and family can bring joy into your life; otherwise, what is the point of success if you have to celebrate it alone...
>
> **99**
>
> **SANDHYA JANE**
> AUTHOR

@Sandhyajane.com

Sandhya Jane

"

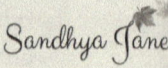

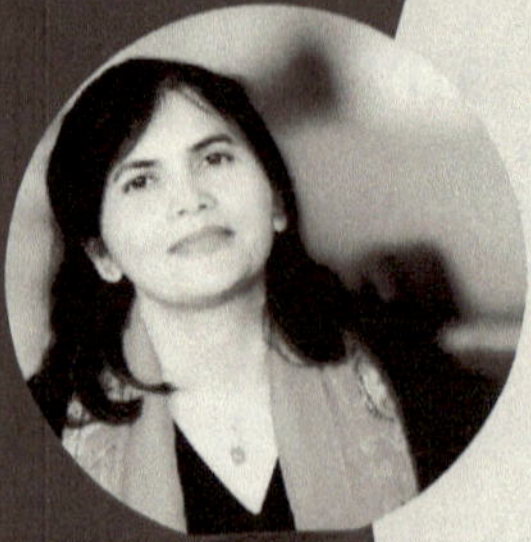

You can never start your business until you have the courage to accept challenges and uncertainties.

"

SANDHYA JANE

AUTHOR

@Sandhyajane.com

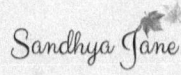

> The day you learn to compliment others and celebrate their success genuinely, that will be the last day of your loneliness...

SANDHYA JANE
AUTHOR

@Sandhyajane.com

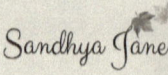
Sandhya Jane

> **"**
>
> Excessive pride will blind you; the way you cannot see other buildings or people on the street from the top of your building.
>
> **"**
>
> **SANDHYA JANE**
> AUTHOR

@Sandhyajane.com

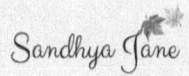

> If we could express our love as easily as our anger, the world would be different.

SANDHYA JANE
AUTHOR

@Sandhyajane.com

Sandhya Jane

> Sharing a laugh or a pain is the most significant part of life. If you have someone, you are lucky; if you have more than one, you are even luckier.
>
> Build your circle.

SANDHYA JANE
AUTHOR

@Sandhyajane.com

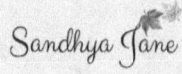

> When meeting new people, stick to the generic topics at the beginning; to reach to the inner core, you need to put some efforts together and build the relationship.

SANDHYA JANE
AUTHOR

@Sandhyajane.com

Sandhya Jane

— 99 —

Watch your mother and father working at home, watch your senior colleagues working at the office; it will reduce your learning curve and give you more time to focus on new areas/ideas.

— 99 —

SANDHYA JANE
AUTHOR

@Sandhyajane.com

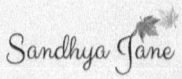

> Read books on the topics you wish to be an expert on; it will reduce your learning curve and improve your creative abilities.

SANDHYA JANE
AUTHOR

@Sandhyajane.com

Sandhya Jane

> Relationship is not a glass that once broken, cannot be rejoined; just like the Japanese concept of 'Kintsugi', once anything is shattered, you can always transform it into an unique piece by joining the broken pieces with gold.
>
> This beautiful and unique relationship will have its own history to be proud of.

SANDHYA JANE
AUTHOR

@Sandhyajane.com

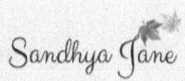

Sandhya Jane

> Who said discipline was not important? Can a book be produced without an author sitting at a desk, writing and editing for hours? Can a sculpture be completed without an artist working diligently on it for hours? Can a project be delivered if the manager and team aren't involved wholeheartedly? 1/2

SANDHYA JANE
AUTHOR

@Sandhyajane.com

Sandhya Jane

> Can a movie be completed without all the members coming together and working in a strict environment for hours?
>
> So, conscious and continuous efforts are important to complete the assignment and series of successfully completed assignments needed to build your professional career and brand. 2/2

SANDHYA JANE
AUTHOR

@Sandhyajane.com

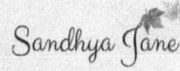

> Before making a moon your satellite, you should first find out how many planets revolve around that moon.

SANDHYA JANE
AUTHOR

@Sandhyajane.com

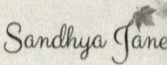

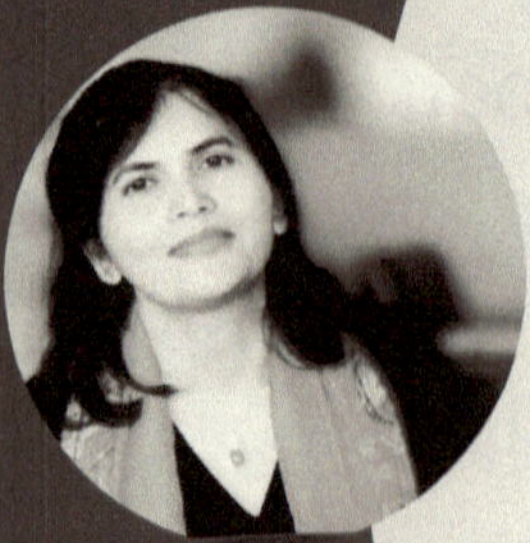

> **"**
> If scholars do not take a stand against injustice, society will soon lose peace.
> **"**

SANDHYA JANE
AUTHOR

@Sandhyajane.com

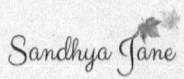

> **"**
> Wisdom is - accepting the outcome as a part of your destiny, when you could not change the outcome; and appreciating your efforts and destiny when you achieved the desired outcome...
> **"**

SANDHYA JANE
AUTHOR

@Sandhyajane.com

Sandhya Jane

> **"**
>
> If you make your daily chores such as cooking, cleaning, exercising, reading, organizing etc., a part of your daily routine, your life will always be in order.
>
> **"**
>
> **SANDHYA JANE**
> AUTHOR

@Sandhyajane.com

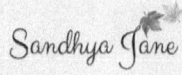

> We need to learn to accept and accommodate shortcomings before building a successful relationship.

SANDHYA JANE
AUTHOR

@Sandhyajane.com

Sandhya Jane

> **A mistake enhances your experience and experience reduces your mistakes.**

SANDHYA JANE
AUTHOR

@Sandhyajane.com

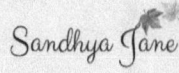

> It takes a second to click a photo; it takes a lifetime to build an image...

SANDHYA JANE
AUTHOR

@Sandhyajane.com

Sandhya Jane

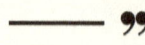

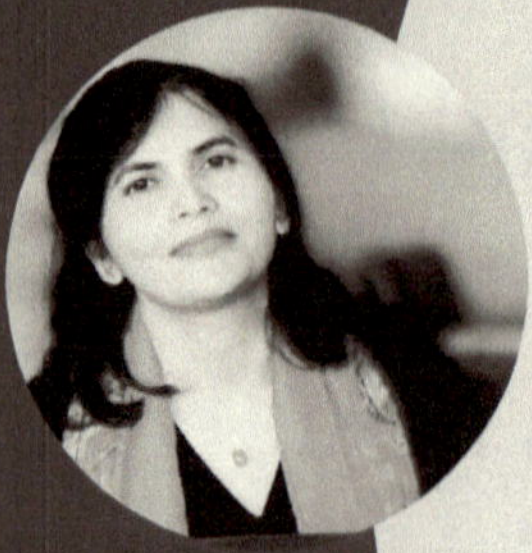

The key to living a happy life is to find happiness in the small things in life; and the second most imperative thing is to not hold on to the happiness of the past.

SANDHYA JANE

AUTHOR

@Sandhyajane.com

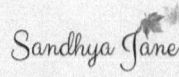

> It doesn't take much struggle to earn the basics of life, such as food, clothes, shelter, etc. However, it does take a great dealof struggle and stress to fulfill one's endless greed.

SANDHYA JANE
AUTHOR

@Sandhyajane.com

Sandhya Jane

> **"**
> If you think it is okay to be untidy, try inviting your office colleagues or your girlfriend or boyfriend over to your home. Ask yourself if you would like to be friends with a filthy person.
> **"**

SANDHYA JANE
AUTHOR

@Sandhyajane.com

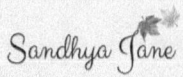

> There is nothing called 'my life' when we have to live in a family or work in an office; there will be certain adjustments as well as accommodations needed to live in social and professional life.

SANDHYA JANE
AUTHOR

@Sandhyajane.com

Sandhya Jane

> What is poison?
> Having anything more than we need can become poison; excess money, power, beauty, or ego can be poisonous and turn you into a demon if you don't manage them well..

SANDHYA JANE
AUTHOR

@Sandhyajane.com

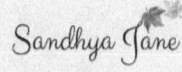

> We do what we want to do; however, the outcome depends on what God wishes us to do...

SANDHYA JANE
AUTHOR

@Sandhyajane.com

Sandhya Jane

> **" "**
>
> A pocket full of money can show you the world, but an empty pocket gives you the experience of the world.
>
> **" "**
>
> **SANDHYA JANE**
> AUTHOR

@Sandhyajane.com

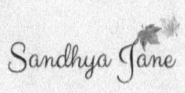

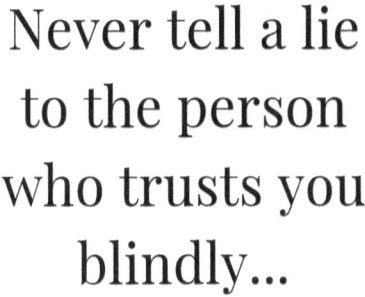

> Never tell a lie to the person who trusts you blindly...

SANDHYA JANE
AUTHOR

@Sandhyajane.com

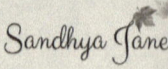

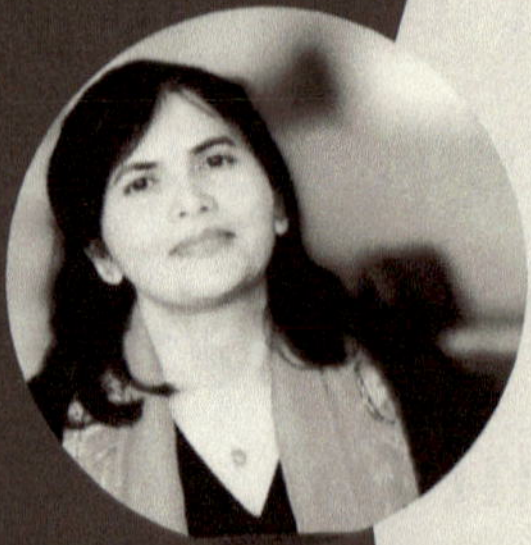

> **"**
>
> The moment a doubt enters your mind, love and trust leave you...
>
> **"**
>
> **SANDHYA JANE**
> AUTHOR

@Sandhyajane.com

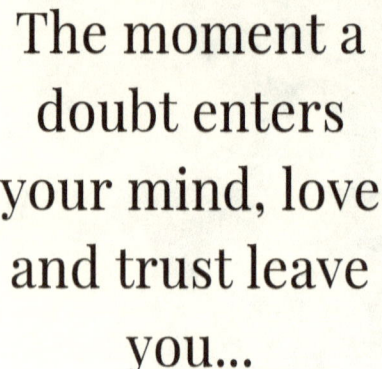

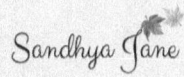

> Coincidence brings people into your life, but lack of confidence forces them to leave you.

SANDHYA JANE
AUTHOR

@Sandhyajane.com

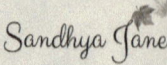
Sandhya Jane

> **99**
>
> The mighty ocean remains within its limits, but a tiny man often crosses his limits.
>
> **99**
>
> **SANDHYA JANE**
> AUTHOR

@Sandhyajane.com

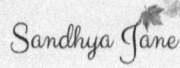

> Life in total is the addition of joys, subtraction of sorrows, multiplication of hard-work, and division of failures....

SANDHYA JANE
AUTHOR

@Sandhyajane.com

Sandhya Jane

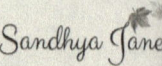

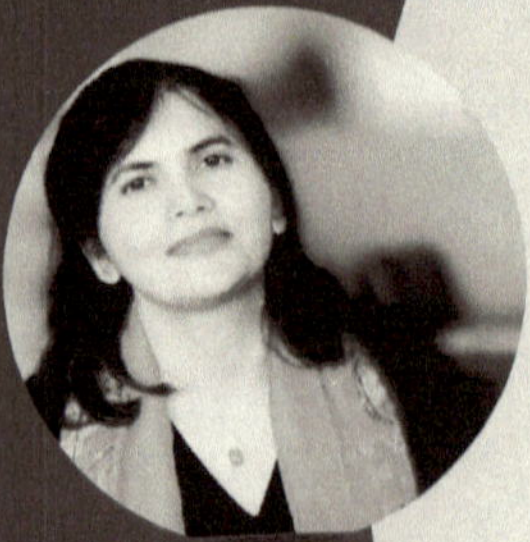

Believe in God or a Creator. Otherwise, you cannot possibly imagine how advanced science and technology can be used to recreate such complex creatures, a perfect environment, and a perfect balance for them to coexist.

SANDHYA JANE
AUTHOR

@Sandhyajane.com

> Some people come into our lives and touch our hearts with their beautiful thoughts and kind behavior; we must value these people as diamonds because they are rare.

SANDHYA JANE
AUTHOR

@Sandhyajane.com

Sandhya Jane

> God does not need followers, or worst case, followers who compel others to follow him; that is an illusion created by institutions that seek to institutionalize your fear and faith.

SANDHYA JANE
AUTHOR

@Sandhyajane.com

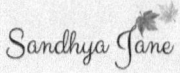

> **Devotion is better than sincerity because devotion is a deep, emotional, and spiritual commitment to a cause that doesn't change with the environment.**
>
> **SANDHYA JANE**
> AUTHOR

@Sandhyajane.com

Sandhya Jane

> "
>
> If life gives you lemons, make lemonade, sell it, and enjoy its profit.
>
> "

SANDHYA JANE
AUTHOR

@Sandhyajane.com

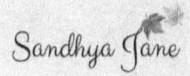

> ❝
> You will find opportunities in every situation.
> ❞
>
> **SANDHYA JANE**
> AUTHOR

@Sandhyajane.com

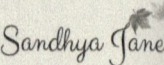

Sandhya Jane

"Unconditional love and devotion are the most valuable gifts you can give your parents."

SANDHYA JANE

AUTHOR

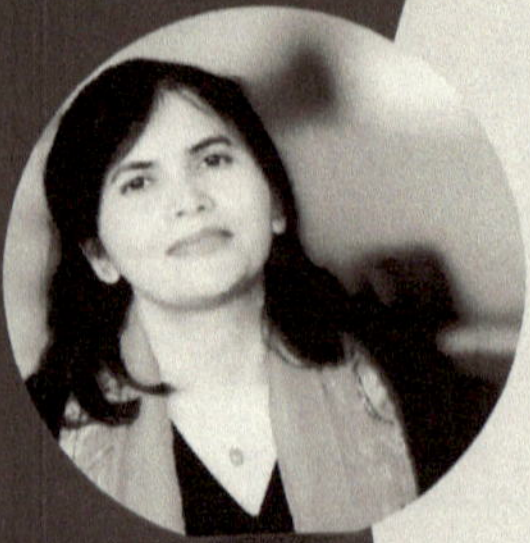

@Sandhyajane.com

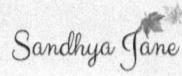

> Embrace life and its experiences with an open mind, and you will sail through it peacefully and successfully.

SANDHYA JANE
AUTHOR

@Sandhyajane.com

Sandhya Jane

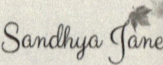

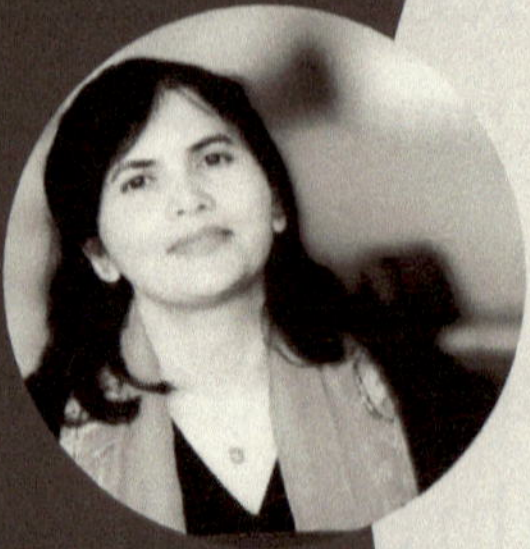

No amount of money or care can be a return gift to your parents, as nothing can substitute their parenting gift to you.

SANDHYA JANE

AUTHOR

@Sandhyajane.com

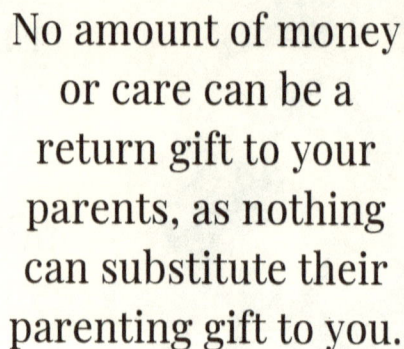

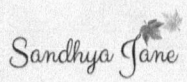

> If you cannot avoid a warning that is generated by your gadget before something goes wrong with it, how can you avoid the warning that is generated by parents out of genuine concern and care as well as their own personal experiences?

SANDHYA JANE
AUTHOR

@Sandhyajane.com

Sandhya Jane

> **99**
>
> Life is not rosy; however we have the option to enjoy a little topsy-turvy, some adventure and a few uncertainties.
>
> **99**
>
> **SANDHYA JANE**
> AUTHOR

@Sandhyajane.com

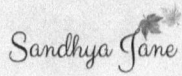

> "
> Don't count on 100 when you get angry, because it suppresses it; just walk away from the situation when it is about to get heated, and return back only when you are ready to continue peacefully. Suppressing anger will do more harm than delaying the situation.
> "

SANDHYA JANE
AUTHOR

@Sandhyajane.com

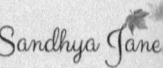

> **❞**
>
> 'I, me, myself' is an unsustainable and selfish idea; if you find such a person, run, run and run away... Life is about 'us'. What you do for yourself to be worthy of your family, your society and your nation is far more meaningful than wearing a fancy dress to a night club to attract a few undeserving people for a moment.
> **Is it worth it?**
>
> **❞**
>
> **SANDHYA JANE**
> AUTHOR

@Sandhyajane.com

> Apologizing sincerely in public after making mistakes requires both courage and conviction; it is not everyone's cup of tea...

SANDHYA JANE
AUTHOR

@Sandhyajane.com

Sandhya Jane

> **"**
>
> People who live in our hearts, care for them; people who leave our hearts, be careful of them...
>
> **"**

SANDHYA JANE
AUTHOR

@Sandhyajane.com

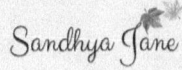

> Open your eyes before you close them; it is important to change the course of your life.

SANDHYA JANE
AUTHOR

@Sandhyajane.com

Sandhya Jane

> **"**
>
> Meaning of Life:
> Death is an ultimate truth after you are born, and you cannot change that; what you do between birth and death is certainly in your control. So, choose this time and your priorities wisely.
>
> **"**
>
> **SANDHYA JANE**
> AUTHOR

@Sandhyajane.com

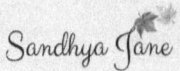

> As children play with their friends, they face a myriad of emotions including love, rejection, hatred, acceptance, let-go, etc., which provides them with an emotional outlet and makes them happy. Adults tend to dump all these emotions inside their hearts and live in misery. Fighting, making up, acceptances, rejections, love, hatred, letting go, these are all part of life and part of the secret of long-term relationships.

SANDHYA JANE
AUTHOR

@Sandhyajane.com

Sandhya Jane

"

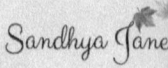

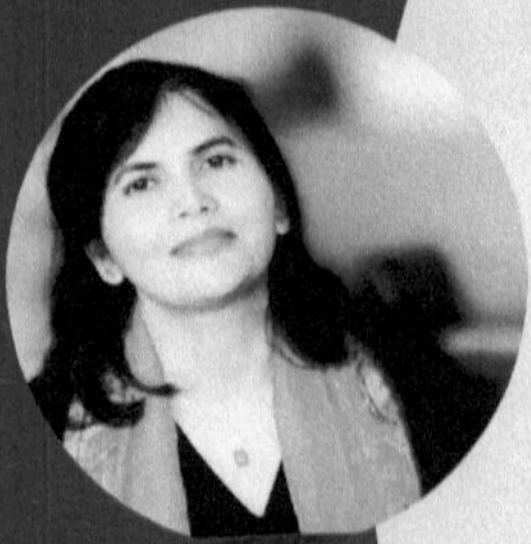

When you change with the situation, so does another person; accept this.

"

SANDHYA JANE

AUTHOR

@Sandhyajane.com

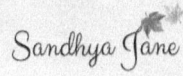

> **99**
>
> Joy and blessings multiply when you give them to others...
>
> **99**
>
> SANDHYA JANE
> AUTHOR

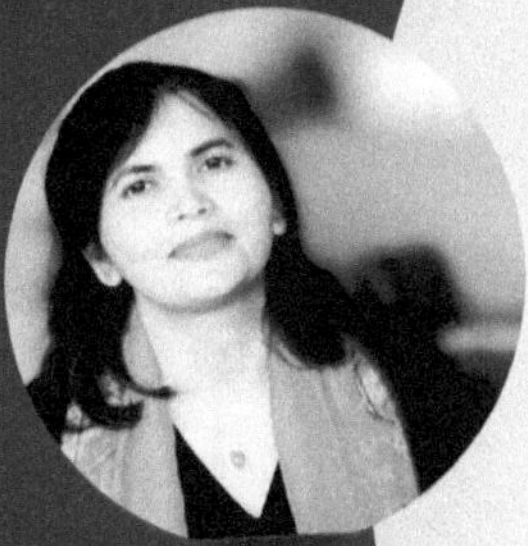

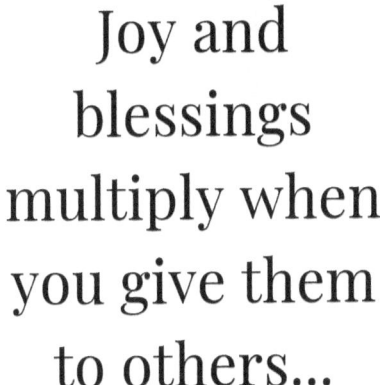

@Sandhyajane.com

Sandhya Jane

> **"**
>
> If you don't close the door to the past, you can't open the door to the future.
>
> **"**
>
> **SANDHYA JANE**
> AUTHOR

@Sandhyajane.com

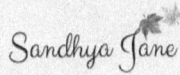

> **Karma:**
> This life is about yours and your parents' karma; but what you do in this life will set the tone for this and for the next life.
>
> **SANDHYA JANE**
> AUTHOR

@Sandhyajane.com

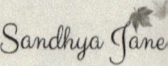

> **"**
>
> The Perfect Life:
> Life is not perfect for anyone; find beauty in your own life. Similar to 'cha-no-yu' (the tea ceremony) of fifteenth-century Japan, 'wabi-sabi' is an aesthetic that finds beauty in imperfection, impermanence, and incompleteness.
>
> **"**
>
> **SANDHYA JANE**
> AUTHOR

@Sandhyajane.com

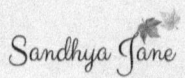

> Most relationships can be worked out if violence is not involved. Everyone has both positive qualities and shortcomings.
> To create a lasting relationship, you need to accept both good qualities as well as shortcomings in the other person.

SANDHYA JANE
AUTHOR

@Sandhyajane.com

Sandhya Jane

> The relationship is doomed sooner or later when one of them tries to change the other completely. Marriage is the union of two families, since other family members will be involved in the family circle or in the couple's heads.

SANDHYA JANE
AUTHOR

@Sandhyajane.com

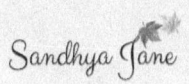

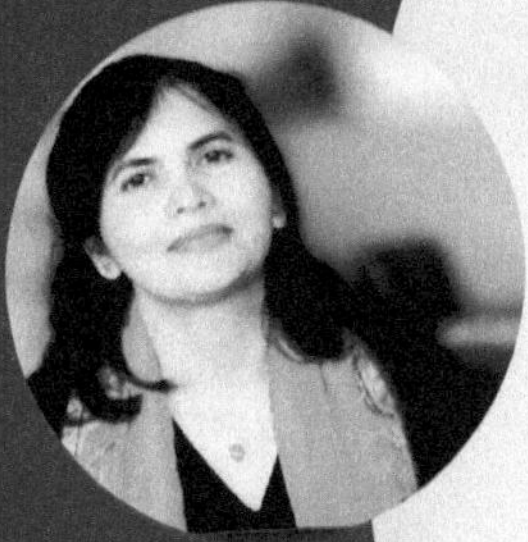

> **"**
>
> Every soul comes to this world with a purpose; find your purpose and fulfill it.
>
> **"**
>
> **SANDHYA JANE**
> AUTHOR & SPEAKER

@Sandhyajane.com

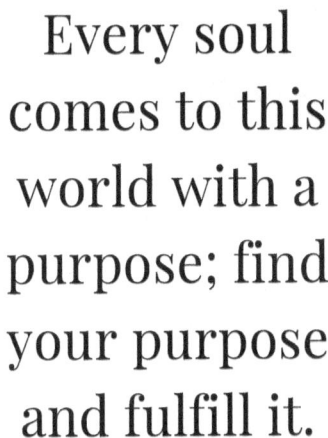

Sandhya Jane

> **99**
>
> In life, both joy and sorrow are part of the cycle, but only God knows how much distance a person will have between each cycle.
>
> **99**

SANDHYA JANE
AUTHOR & SPEAKER

@Sandhyajane.com

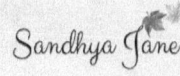

> There is no concept of absolute privacy unless you prefer to live in a jungle. In the broader interest of society, the need for security always triumphs over private privacy.

SANDHYA JANE
AUTHOR & SPEAKER

@Sandhyajane.com

Sandhya Jane

> 99
>
> There is absolutely no guarantee that future partner will be better than current partner as he may come with different types of good qualities as well as shortcomings. Pause. Think. Act.
>
> 99
>
> **SANDHYA JANE**
> AUTHOR & SPEAKER

@Sandhyajane.com

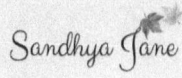

> Parents, brothers, sisters, parents-in-law sister-in-law, brother-in-law etc., are part of the family. Do keep them in inner circle as much as possible. This way, you don't have to live a lonely life.

SANDHYA JANE
AUTHOR & SPEAKER

@Sandhyajane.com

Sandhya Jane

> Seeing an octogenarian struggling to get groceries alone in a supermarket indicates a breakdown of society. Ideally, they should be either at home or in a care center under the supervision of a caretaker.

SANDHYA JANE
AUTHOR & SPEAKER

@Sandhyajane.com

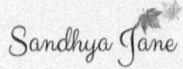

> If you want to do something for society, consider adopting an elderly person or offering him/her care and company in old age. In return, you will have access to his/her company and learn from real life experiences.
> This will help rebuild society to some extend.
> This can happen only if we give up on insisting on spending on expensive items or trips or other unnecessary things in life.

SANDHYA JANE
AUTHOR & SPEAKER

@Sandhyajane.com

Sandhya Jane

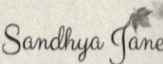

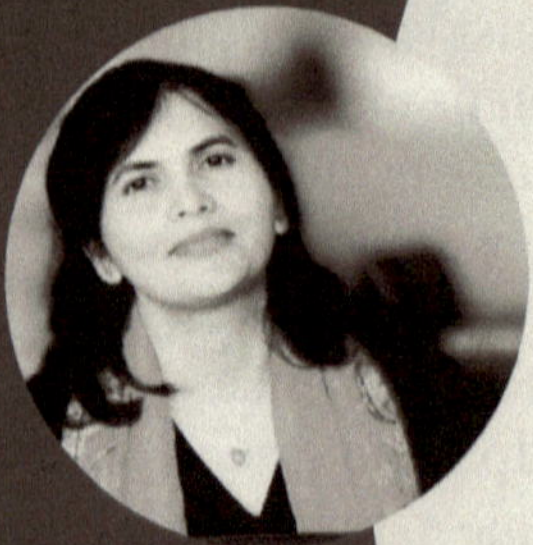

A disturbed mind can get lost in the light; and a peaceful mind can find a path in darkness.

SANDHYA JANE
AUTHOR & SPEAKER

@Sandhyajane.com

> If you can bring a smile to others' faces, you have found the meaning of life.

SANDHYA JANE
AUTHOR & SPEAKER

@Sandhyajane.com

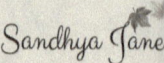

Sandhya Jane

"

Being happy in strangers' company is better than being sad in known company.

"

SANDHYA JANE

AUTHOR & SPEAKER

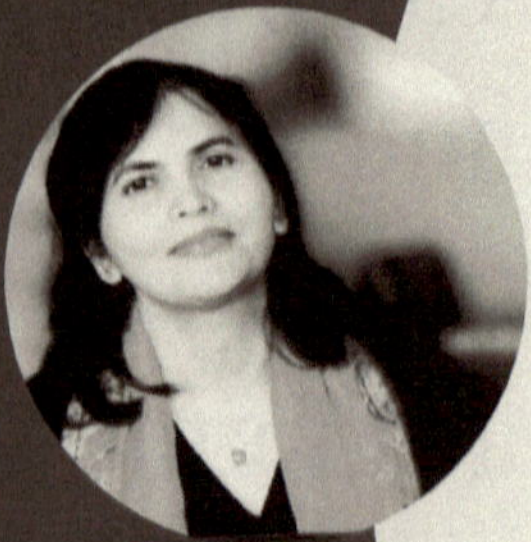

@Sandhyajane.com

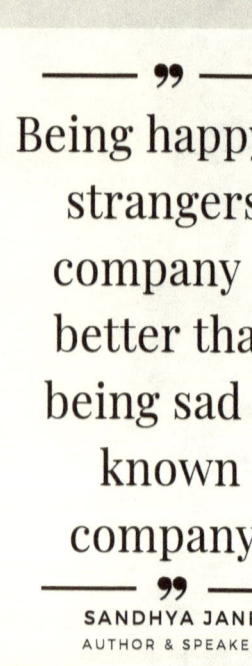

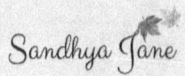

Sandhya Jane

> A day invested in 'self' as well as in 'others' is the 'best day'; if we add more such 'best days', it will eventually become the best life...

SANDHYA JANE
AUTHOR & SPEAKER

@Sandhyajane.com

Sandhya Jane

> Relationships are built by investing efforts and time; and broken by impulse or greed.

SANDHYA JANE
AUTHOR & SPEAKER

@Sandhyajane.com

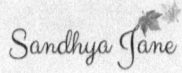
Sandhya Jane

> A wicked person will always create hindrances to others' work; otherwise, a good person can survive on good work.

SANDHYA JANE
AUTHOR & SPEAKER

@Sandhyajane.com

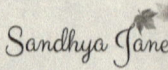

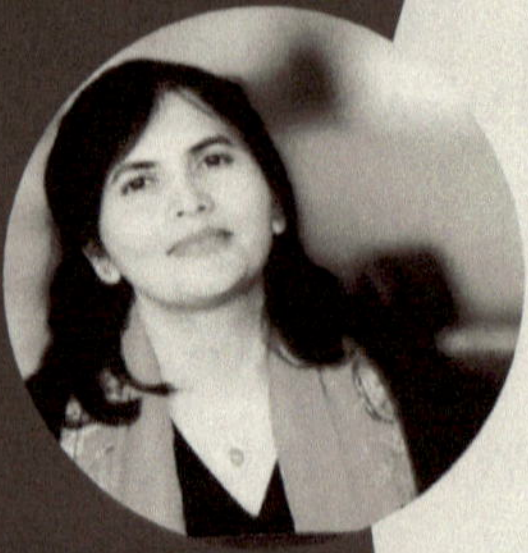

Sandhya Jane

Diya Tale andhera: there is darkness below the lamp.
- Hindu proverb.

SANDHYA JANE
AUTHOR & SPEAKER

@Sandhyajane.com

> Adh-jal ghaghari chhalkat jaye – the half-full pot spills more water. Thus, someone with half the knowledge or a small amount of wealth boasts more than someone with full knowledge or abundant wealth.

SANDHYA JANE
AUTHOR & SPEAKER

@Sandhyajane.com

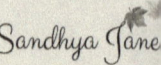

> **99**
>
> The best way to come out of grief is to know what you can do and what you cannot, and know the difference between both. Secondly, how to make your life more meaningful. Once you learn the latter part, you may find the loss is insignificant.
>
> **99**

SANDHYA JANE
AUTHOR & SPEAKER

@Sandhyajane.com

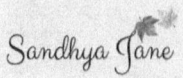

> **"**
>
> A donation becomes corrupt when you humiliate the recipient either by insulting, giving it late, giving face to face, speaking harsh words while giving or repenting after giving.
>
> **"**
>
> **SANDHYA JANE**
> AUTHOR & SPEAKER

@Sandhyajane.com

Sandhya Jane

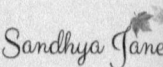

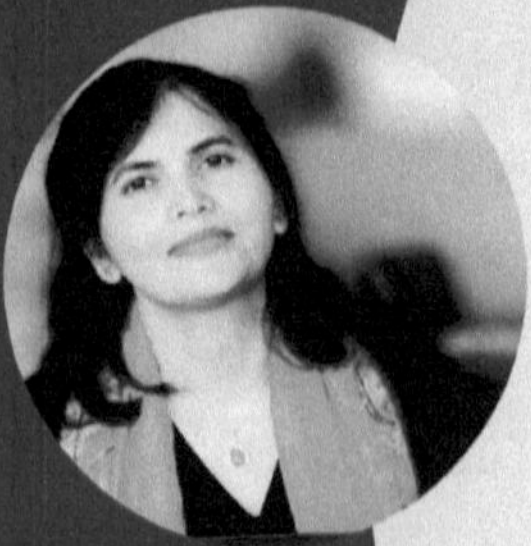

Like children, find your emotional outlets through sports, hobbies or clubs. You will feel lighter and happier when your emotional trash is emptied regularly.

SANDHYA JANE

AUTHOR & SPEAKER

@Sandhyajane.com

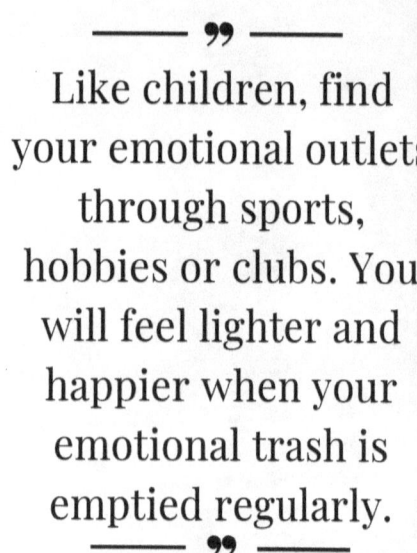

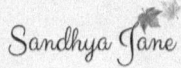

> Give yourself some time to work – it is the source of creating success;
>
> Give yourself some time to think – it is the source of generating ideas;
>
> Give yourself some time for sports – it is the secret of your youthfulness;
>
> Give yourself sometime for reading – it is the source of your knowledge;
>
> Give yourself some time for yourself – it is the source of being alive
>
> Give yourself some time for others – it is the source of creating a meaningful life…

SANDHYA JANE
AUTHOR & SPEAKER

@Sandhyajane.com

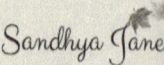

Sandhya Jane

”

Happiness doesn’t need a luxury place; it needs happy heart.

”

SANDHYA JANE
AUTHOR & SPEAKER

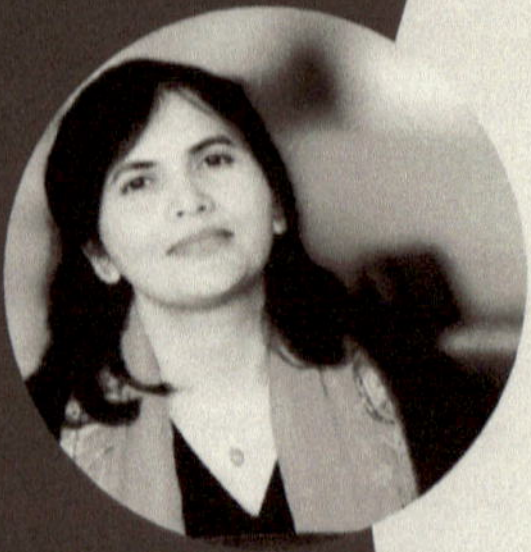

@Sandhyajane.com

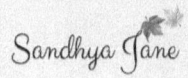

Sandhya Jane

> **❞**
>
> If no one is jealous of you, it means you are not doing anything significant in your life.
>
> **❞**

SANDHYA JANE
AUTHOR & SPEAKER

@Sandhyajane.com

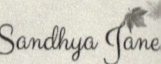

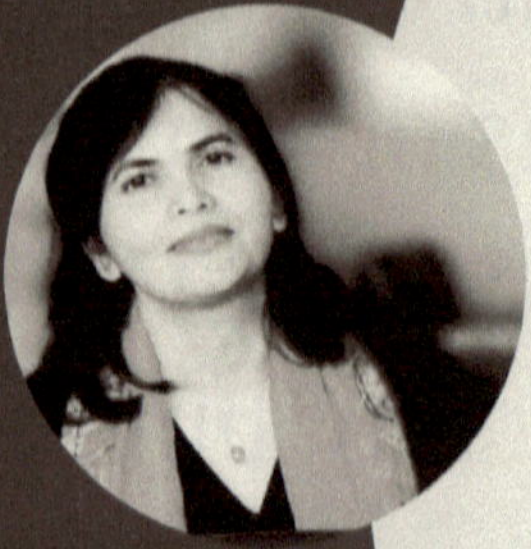

> ❞
>
> Don't trust a cat with milk and don't trust a thief with money.
>
> ❞
>
> **SANDHYA JANE**
> AUTHOR & SPEAKER

@Sandhyajane.com

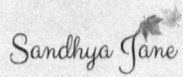

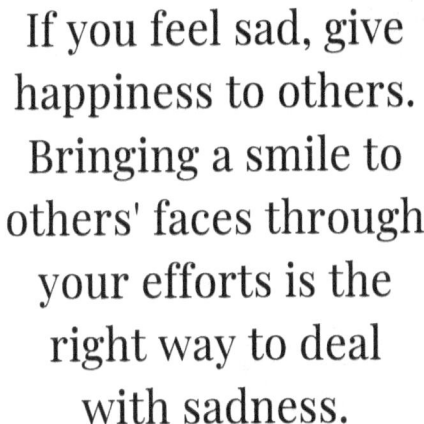

> If you feel sad, give happiness to others. Bringing a smile to others' faces through your efforts is the right way to deal with sadness.
>
> **SANDHYA JANE**
> AUTHOR & SPEAKER

@Sandhyajane.com

Sandhya Jane

> **"**
>
> Every pig enjoys shit; so, don't think of wrestling with a pig...
>
> **"**
>
> **SANDHYA JANE**
> AUTHOR & SPEAKER

@Sandhyajane.com

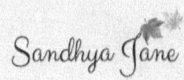

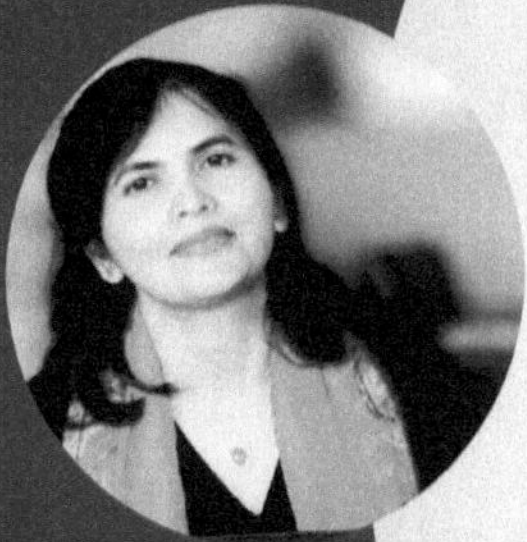

> There is lots of mystery and misery in the world; don't add to it, but make an effort to reduce it.

SANDHYA JANE
AUTHOR & SPEAKER

@Sandhyajane.com

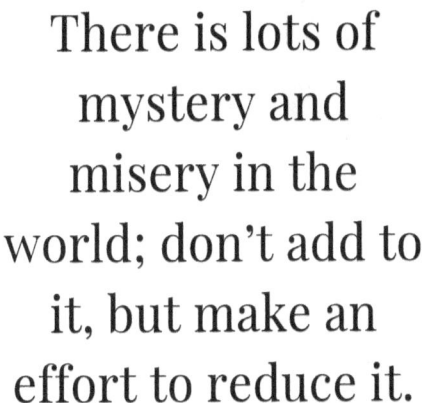

Sandhya Jane

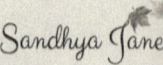

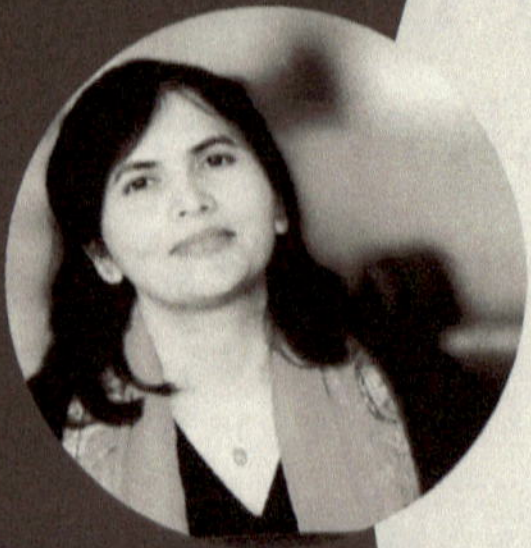

There is no friend or enemy; only your conduct and intent causes people to become your friends or enemies.

SANDHYA JANE

AUTHOR & SPEAKER

@Sandhyajane.com

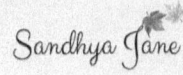

> Peace prevails in our lives when we keep our mind, body and spirit in sync both in action as well as in thoughts...

SANDHYA JANE
AUTHOR & SPEAKER

@Sandhyajane.com

Sandhya Jane

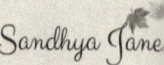

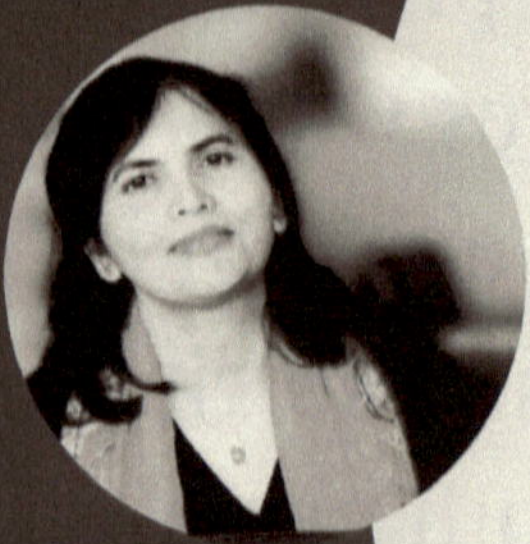

When a machine becomes rusty, it makes noise; similarly, when your 'power' becomes rusty, your tongue makes noise...

SANDHYA JANE
AUTHOR & SPEAKER

@Sandhyajane.com

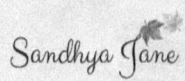

> When **love** is in your heart, you become **kind**;
> When **respect** is in your heart, you become **humble**;
> When **anger** is in your heart, you become **hostile**;
> When **doubt** is in your heart, you become **fearful**.
> **You just reflect on what is inside you.**

SANDHYA JANE
AUTHOR & SPEAKER

@Sandhyajane.com

Sandhya Jane

> It is not size or beauty or power; it is 'the mettle' that differentiates leaders from followers.

SANDHYA JANE
AUTHOR & SPEAKER

@Sandhyajane.com

Sandhya Jane

> **"**
>
> When a relationship brings you down constantly, you must let it go. A positive relationship lifts you, cares for you, and inspires you, and above all, it values you and your priorities.
>
> **"**
>
> **SANDHYA JANE**
> AUTHOR & SPEAKER

@Sandhyajane.com

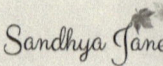

Sandhya Jane

"

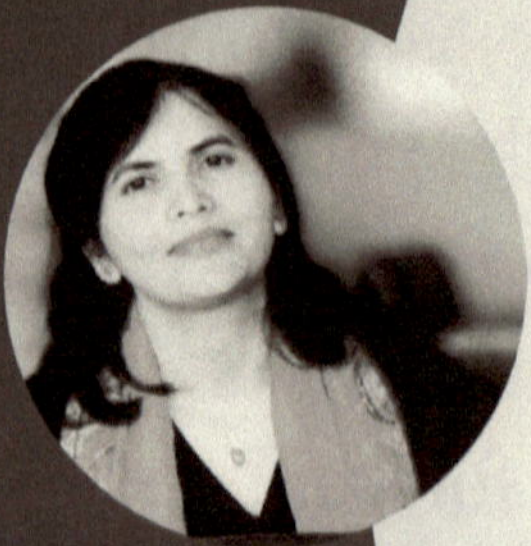

Life is short; so, make most of it.

"

SANDHYA JANE

AUTHOR & SPEAKER

@Sandhyajane.com

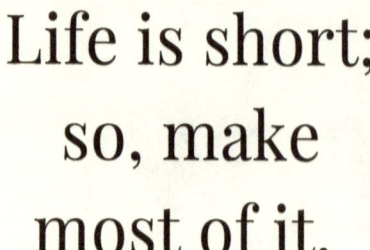

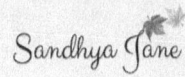

> Some adversaries in life do not come to test you; rather, they come to test your real friends and their support during the crisis...

SANDHYA JANE
AUTHOR & SPEAKER

@Sandhyajane.com

Sandhya Jane

> **99**
>
> The best things in life, such as winter sun, morning breeze, starry nights, walking on the grass, dancing in the rain, watching sunsets on the beach... all these pleasures are free in life; all we need to do is go out, enjoy them, and immerse ourselves in them.
>
> **99**
>
> **SANDHYA JANE**
> AUTHOR & SPEAKER

@Sandhyajane.com

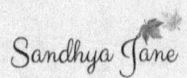

> **"**
> Each person has unlimited possibilities; if you can discover some of them, you can have a positive impact on your life and the world around you.
> **"**
>
> **SANDHYA JANE**
> AUTHOR & SPEAKER

@Sandhyajane.com

Sandhya Jane

> **99**
>
> What is fear? It is discomfort caused by a thought of facing uncertainties. If you calculate the most disastrous possible outcome in any given situation, you will know what the limits are and what you can achieve. That will help you understand your uncertainties and drive away your fears.
>
> **99**

SANDHYA JANE
AUTHOR & SPEAKER

@Sandhyajane.com

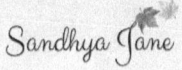

Sandhya Jane

"

Life is uncertain; the only way to make it better is to enjoy each moment of life without wasting it on unnecessary things.

"

SANDHYA JANE
AUTHOR & SPEAKER

@Sandhyajane.com

Sandhya Jane

> Life cannot be changed completely in one day...but with patience and perseverance, it can be changed 'one day'.

SANDHYA JANE
AUTHOR & SPEAKER

@Sandhyajane.com

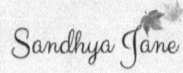

> **Faith and force are both important in life; the key is to know which one to use when...**
>
> **SANDHYA JANE**
> AUTHOR & SPEAKER

@Sandhyajane.com

Sandhya Jane

"

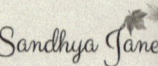

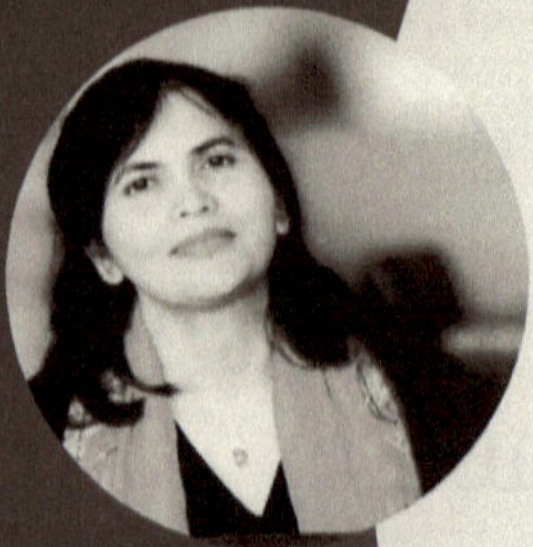

You can collect many friends by hiding your reality; but you can earn a few genuine friends by showing your reality.

"

SANDHYA JANE
AUTHOR & SPEAKER

@Sandhyajane.com

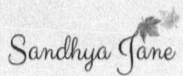

> The most valuable gifts we can offer our children are:
> - Time: Invest in time together regularly.
> - Teaching: Teaching meaningful and useful things in life
> - Tradition: Introducing and participating in the traditions of the family and the community to which we belong

SANDHYA JANE
AUTHOR & SPEAKER

@Sandhyajane.com

Sandhya Jane

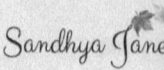

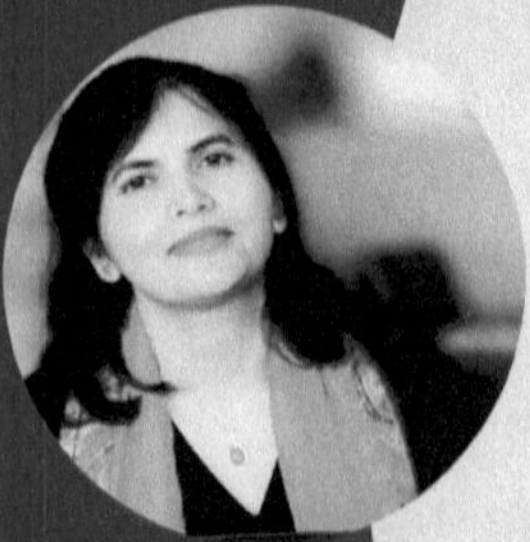

It is necessary to study the past and analyze it once; however, it is absolutely unnecessary to waste your time and energy redoing it over and over again.

SANDHYA JANE
AUTHOR & SPEAKER

@Sandhyajane.com

Sandhya Jane

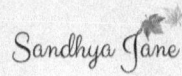

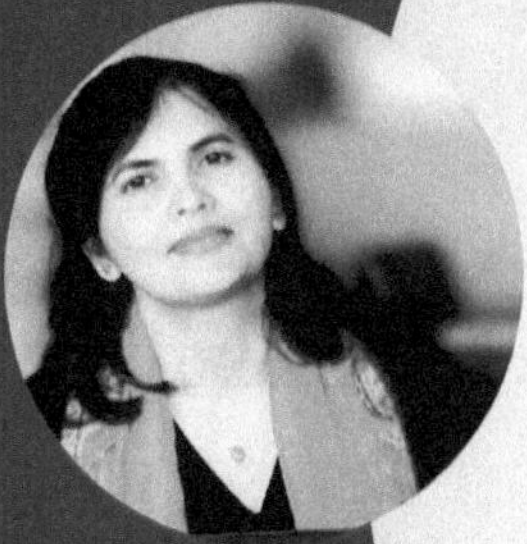

Life is beautiful only if you learn to experience its beauty.

SANDHYA JANE

AUTHOR & SPEAKER

@Sandhyajane.com

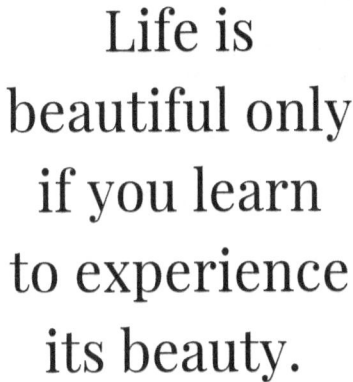

Sandhya Jane

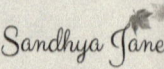

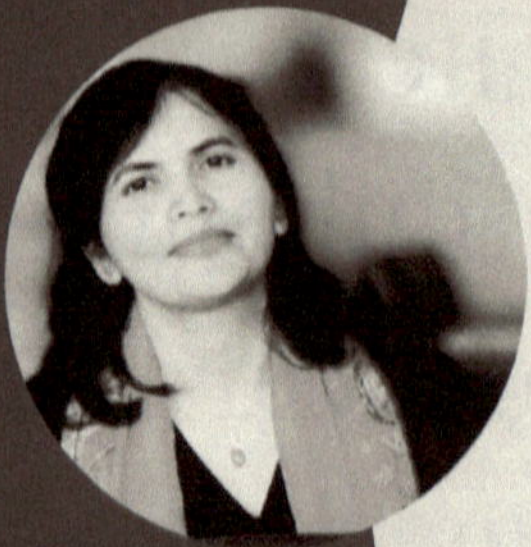

By living in the past or in the future, you waste time and energy needed to accomplish important tasks in the present in order to create a better future.

SANDHYA JANE
AUTHOR & SPEAKER

@Sandhyajane.com

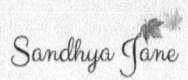

> Life is difficult, including the moment of birth and death. Hence, every living being struggles through survival and hardship; only humans have the capacity to make a difference in others' lives who are less fortunate.

SANDHYA JANE
AUTHOR & SPEAKER

@Sandhyajane.com

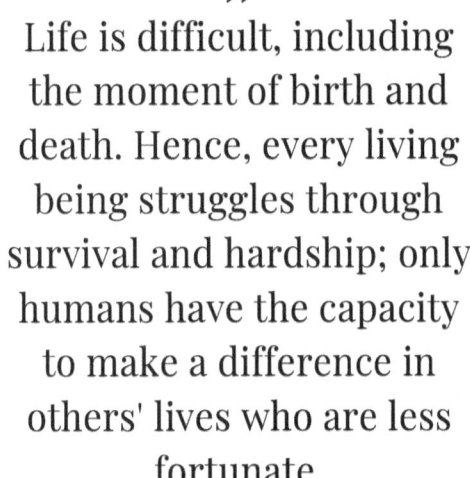

Sandhya Jane

"

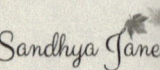

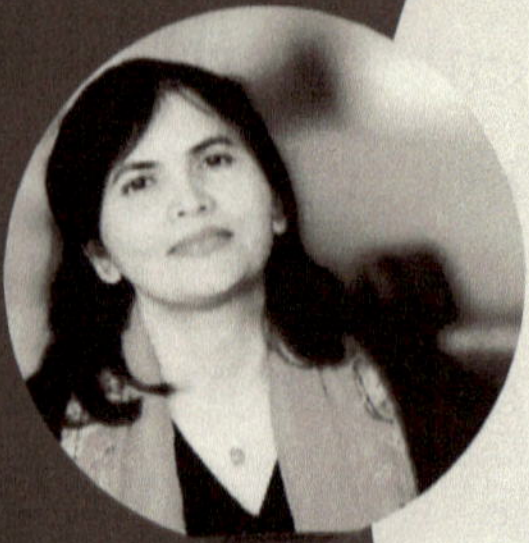

Every relationship is beyond the concept of 50-50 equality as everyone in the relationship has a role t play and every role has its own significance.

"

SANDHYA JANE

AUTHOR & SPEAKER

@Sandhyajane.com

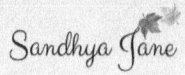

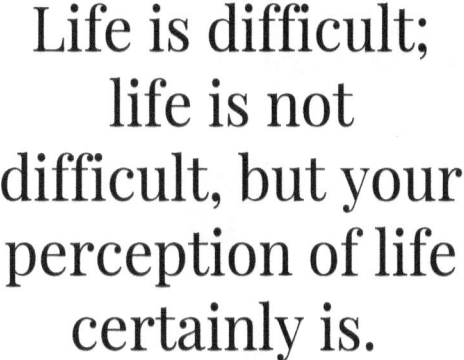

> **Life is difficult; life is not difficult, but your perception of life certainly is.**
>
> **SANDHYA JANE**
> AUTHOR & SPEAKER

@Sandhyajane.com

Sandhya Jane

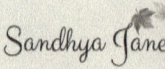

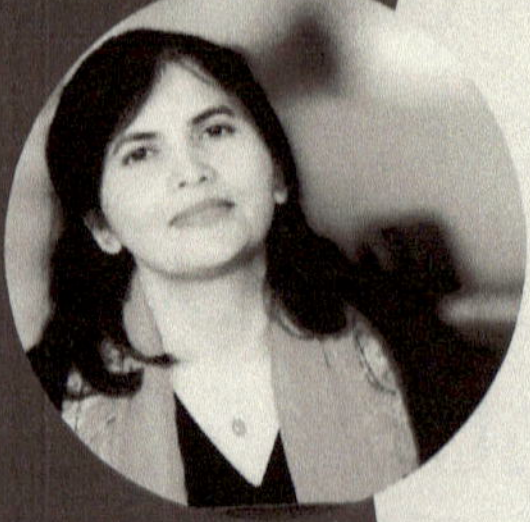

Some people come into your life; others give you the experience of life.

SANDHYA JANE

AUTHOR & SPEAKER

@Sandhyajane.com

Sandhya Jane

> A goal is not bigger than life; if you don't feel that your goal is ideal, choose one that brings you joy and fulfillment...

SANDHYA JANE
AUTHOR & SPEAKER

@Sandhyajane.com

Sandhya Jane

> "A meaningful life can be created in various ways...if you can find it, do it. Otherwise, support someone who is doing meaningful work."

SANDHYA JANE
AUTHOR & SPEAKER

@Sandhyajane.com

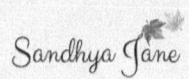

> **❝**
>
> The difference between teen age and middle age is – in teen age, we believe in creating a magic, and in the middle age we understand the concept of magic
>
> **❞**

SANDHYA JANE
AUTHOR & SPEAKER

@Sandhyajane.com

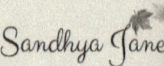

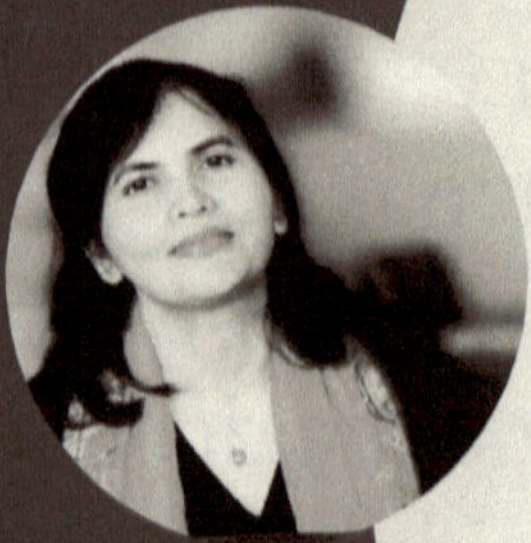

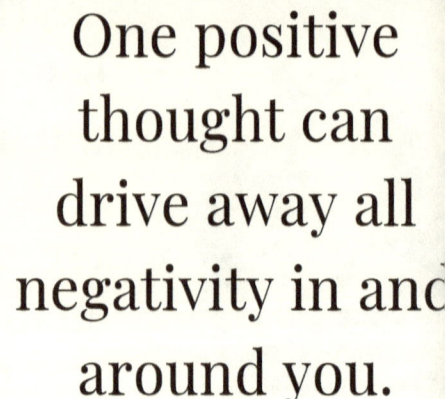

> **One positive thought can drive away all negativity in and around you.**
>
> **SANDHYA JANE**
> AUTHOR & SPEAKER

@Sandhyajane.com

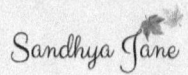

> Life is worthless if you cannot add value to this world.

SANDHYA JANE
AUTHOR & SPEAKER

@Sandhyajane.com

Sandhya Jane

> None can remain neutral in the battle of dharma (justice). Whoever does it, he/she gets aligned with adharma (injustice) automatically.
> - Bhagwat Gita

SANDHYA JANE
AUTHOR & SPEAKER

@Sandhyajane.com

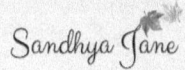

> **Loneliness is a blessing in disguise, provided you know how to utilize this precious time.**
>
> **SANDHYA JANE**
> AUTHOR & SPEAKER

@Sandhyajane.com

Sandhya Jane

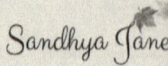

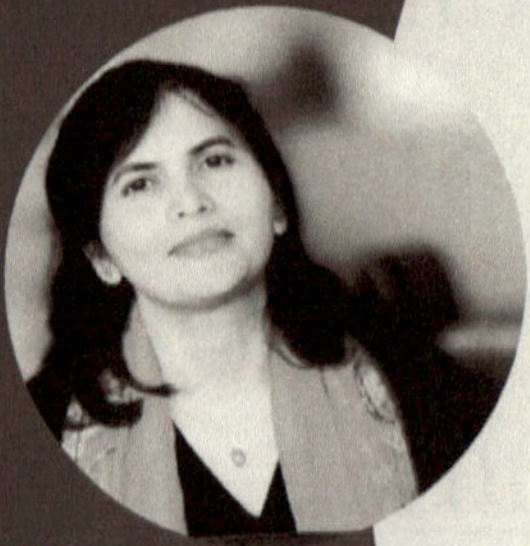

Those who know how to balance their minds will reach the pinnacle of success.

SANDHYA JANE
AUTHOR & SPEAKER

@Sandhyajane.com

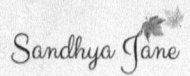

> **"**
>
> Everyone will expect from an 'expectation'; but, no one will be satisfied from a 'satisfaction'.
>
> **"**
>
> **SANDHYA JANE**
> AUTHOR & SPEAKER

@Sandhyajane.com

Sandhya Jane

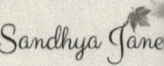

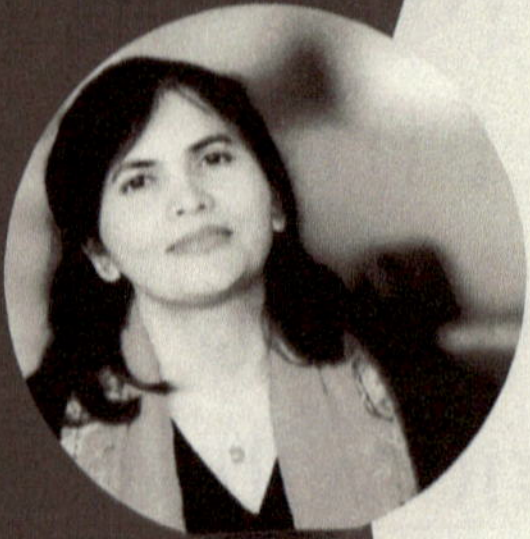

A paper has a power to either become a book and inspire millions or become a trash and get destroyed; similarly, you alone have a power of creating a value of your own life.

SANDHYA JANE

AUTHOR & SPEAKER

@Sandhyajane.com

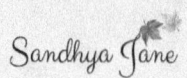

> As we cannot cover the roads with leather, we wear leather shoes to protect our feet; similarly, we cannot change the world; we must change ourselves to become a part of it.

SANDHYA JANE
AUTHOR & SPEAKER

@Sandhyajane.com

Sandhya Jane

> **The only way to live without any enemy is to maintain silence when truth is being defeated...**

SANDHYA JANE
AUTHOR & SPEAKER

@Sandhyajane.com

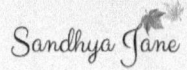

> When you speak ill about others, you forget that you too have weaknesses and others too have the power to speak.

SANDHYA JANE
AUTHOR & SPEAKER

@Sandhyajane.com

Sandhya Jane

”

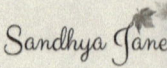

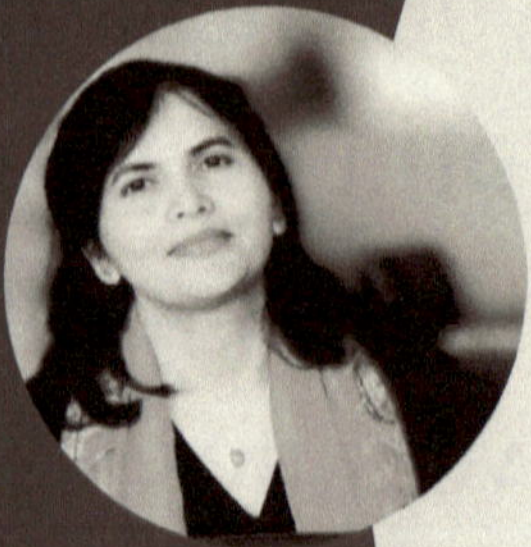

When your mother cries, you become sad; when your father cries, you will be shattered...

”

SANDHYA JANE

AUTHOR & SPEAKER

@Sandhyajane.com

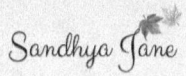
Sandhya Jane

> **Distance doesn't separate two people, but silence does...**

SANDHYA JANE
AUTHOR & SPEAKER

@Sandhyajane.com

Sandhya Jane

> **"**
>
> There is no accurate way to solve the relationship math i.e. when and who to add or subtract. This inaccuracy of math makes us curious and courageous as we change the equation.
>
> **"**
>
> **SANDHYA JANE**
> AUTHOR & SPEAKER

@Sandhyajane.com

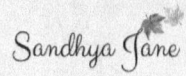

> When you make everyone around you feel valued; you win half of the battle.

SANDHYA JANE
AUTHOR & SPEAKER

@Sandhyajane.com

Sandhya Jane

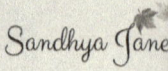

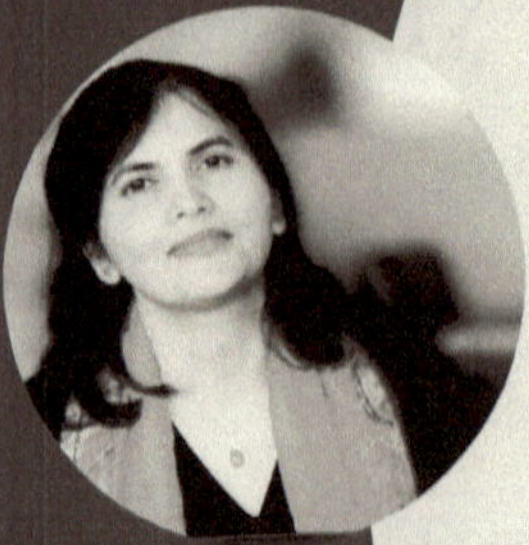

It is easy to forgive someone but it difficult to trust that person again

SANDHYA JANE

AUTHOR & SPEAKER

@Sandhyajane.com

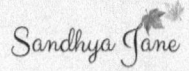
Sandhya Jane

> A relationship without expectations always gives you sweet fruits.

SANDHYA JANE
AUTHOR & SPEAKER

@Sandhyajane.com

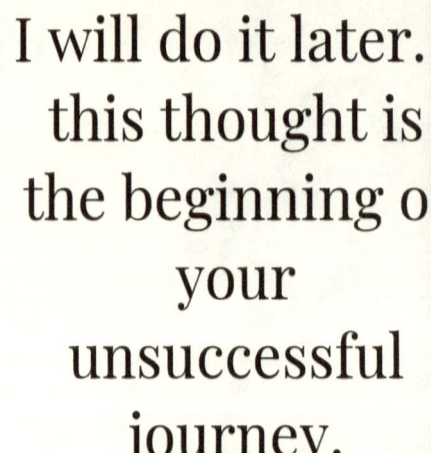

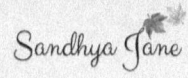

> Your pain may become a cause of others' laughter, but your laughter should never be cause of other's pain.

SANDHYA JANE
AUTHOR & SPEAKER

@Sandhyajane.com

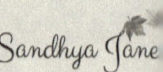

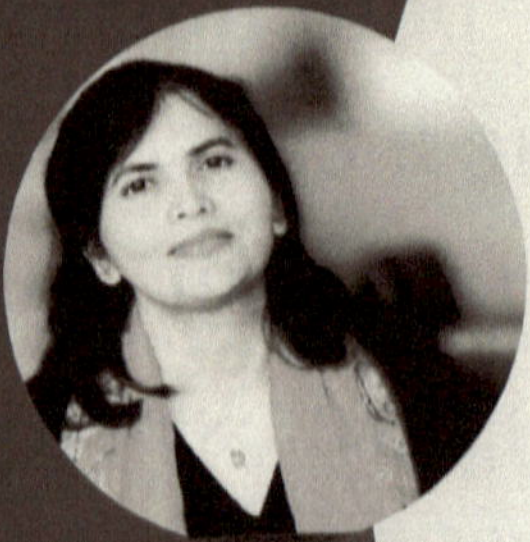

> **A relationship can transform into a joyful kindergarten playground if everyone's strengths and weaknesses are well understood and happily accepted.**

SANDHYA JANE
AUTHOR & SPEAKER

@Sandhyajane.com

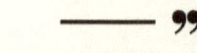

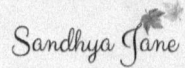

> You may not change the beginning nor you can return to it in the past; but you can always correct the course from this moment to reach your goal...

SANDHYA JANE
AUTHOR & SPEAKER

@Sandhyajane.com

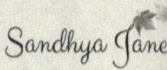
Sandhya Jane

> **Responsibilities:**
> Never give up on your responsibilities. In the end, you will be left with regrets and rejections.

SANDHYA JANE
AUTHOR & SPEAKER

@Sandhyajane.com

> **"**
>
> # Value what you have; admire what you cannot have.
>
> **"**
>
> **SANDHYA JANE**
> AUTHOR & SPEAKER

@Sandhyajane.com

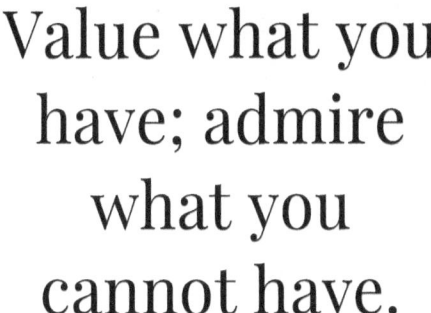

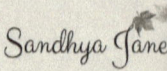

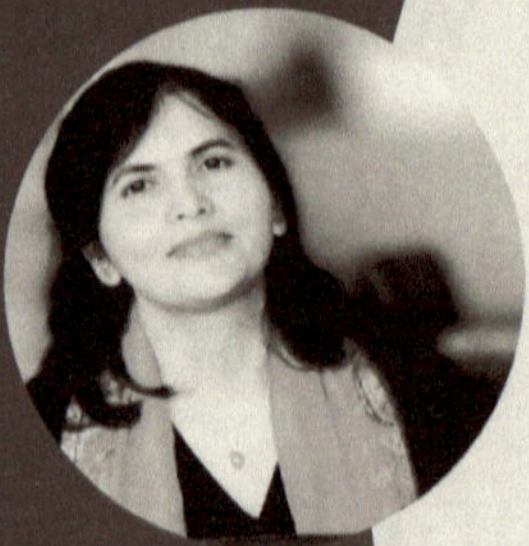

> **"**
>
> Whether you succeed or fail, it depends on your actions and intentions.
>
> **"**
>
> **SANDHYA JANE**
> AUTHOR & SPEAKER

@Sandhyajane.com

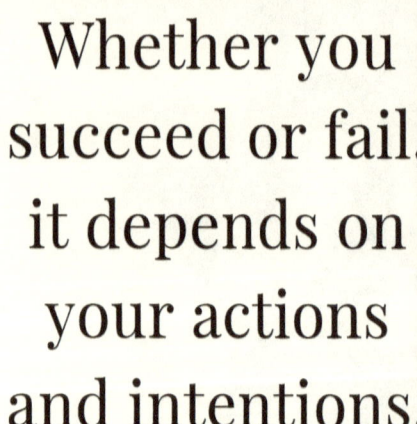

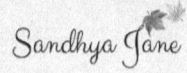

> "
>
> The only way to destroy society is to maintain silence when injustice is done...
>
> "
>
> **SANDHYA JANE**
> AUTHOR & SPEAKER

@Sandhyajane.com

Sandhya Jane

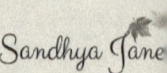

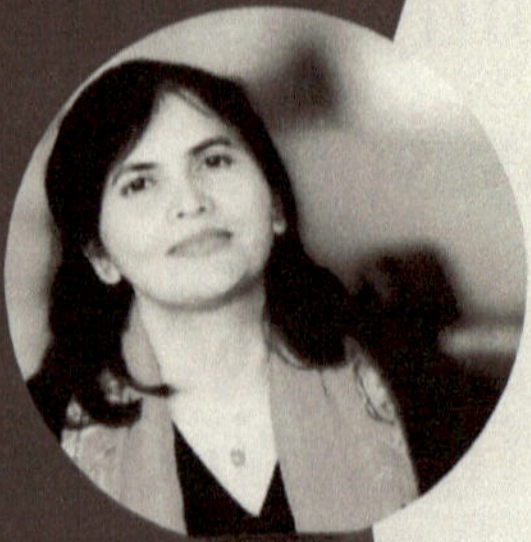

As we do NOT wish to change, we cannot expect others to do so; we must change ourselves first.

SANDHYA JANE
AUTHOR & SPEAKER

@Sandhyajane.com

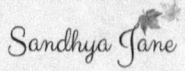
Sandhya Jane

> **"**
>
> Whenever you feel unhappy, watch kids playing, giggling, studying, fighting and preparing themselves for life. Their spirit of life is so powerful that it can change the perception of life.
>
> **"**
>
> **SANDHYA JANE**
> AUTHOR & SPEAKER

@Sandhyajane.com

Sandhya Jane

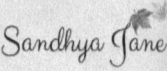

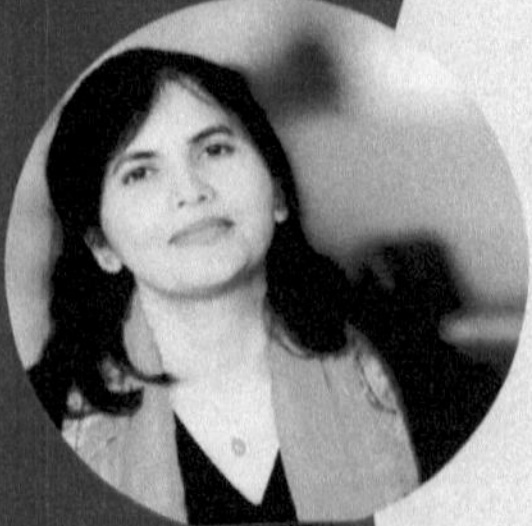

You, alone, know the amount of work, swea and struggle you put into your success; the world sees only the glory of your success.

SANDHYA JANE
AUTHOR & SPEAKER

@Sandhyajane.com

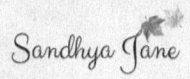

Sandhya Jane

> "
>
> Problems are part of life; when you sort out one, another pops up. All we need to do is continue to live through them without losing the focus on our bigger goals.
>
> "
>
> **SANDHYA JANE**
> AUTHOR & SPEAKER

@Sandhyajane.com

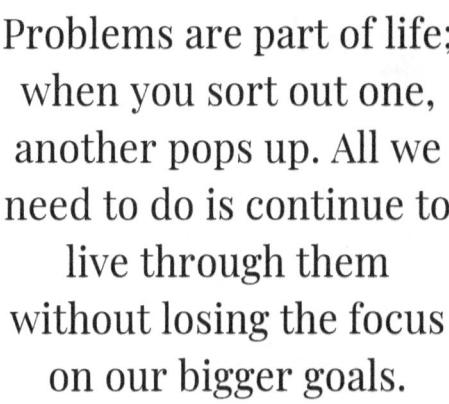

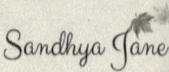

> Responsibility in life makes you get up and get started. In addition, it gives continuity to your work life and adds a sense of fulfillment. Therefore, you should have some serious responsibilities such as taking care of your parents, children, business, employees, etc in your life. The thought that they depend on you will force you to continue with your work.

SANDHYA JANE
AUTHOR & SPEAKER

@Sandhyajane.com

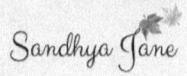

> Whenever you feel your life is worthless, take a walk down the main street and count the number of people working and struggling to survive. Then walk to a poor neighborhood and offer help. Look at the barren land in your city and plant some trees...there are plenty of options for you to make some difference somewhere...

SANDHYA JANE
AUTHOR & SPEAKER

@Sandhyajane.com

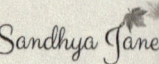

> Happiness is a tempora[ry] state of being; relationships, on the other hand, are permanent, and they ca[n] support and also mak[e] you happy if they are nurtured properly. Choose wisely...

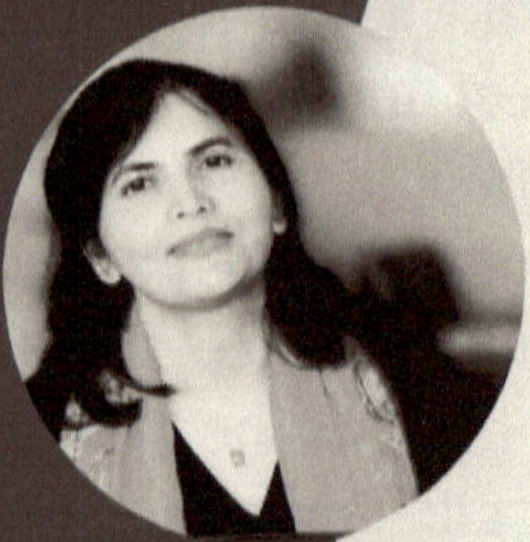

SANDHYA JANE
AUTHOR & SPEAKER

@Sandhyajane.com

Sandhya Jane

> Publicity has evolved into a societal and psychological phenomenon fueled by social media in recent times. Many individuals, regardless of their background, are willing to go to extreme lengths for this publicity. This may involve making unethical and immoral choices, manipulating perceptions with inaccurate information, purchasing items beyond their means, wearing outrageous outfits, and taking unprecedented risks.
>
> Is this pursuit of fame truly more valuable than a career, a relationship, or even life itself?

SANDHYA JANE
AUTHOR & SPEAKER

@Sandhyajane.com

Sandhya Jane

> Acquiring fame without talent, maturity and professional accomplishments is empty since it lacks substance and value.
>
> To acquire fame, the initial stage involves mastering your knowledge and skills, applying them, and uncovering trade secrets before reaching expert status.
>
> By networking and sharing your expertise, fame, wealth, and followers will naturally come your way.

SANDHYA JANE
AUTHOR & SPEAKER

@Sandhyajane.com

ABOUT SANDHYA JANE:

With a Master degree in Information Technologies from the University of Central Missouri, Sandhya Jane has been working for over two decades in the global corporate environment including some of the leading investment banks in USA, India, and Hong Kong.

In addition, she is a successful author with three published books, a mentor to business analysis and project management professionals worldwide, and a sought-after public speaker.

As a writer, she has authored three books: "Second Spring" (contemporary romance), "Sojourn of Life" (poetry), and "Business Analysis: The Question and Answer Book" (a business analysis and project management guide suitable for professional certifications). Sandhya also contributes regularly on technology, management, and motivational topics for top websites and an Indian newspaper.

Her extensive travels for work and leisure have provided her with a unique perspective on various cultures and regions around the world. Presently, she divides her time between Hong Kong, Tokyo, and Mumbai.

@Sandhyajane.com

www.ingramcontent.com/pod-product-compliance
Lightning Source LLC
Chambersburg PA
CBHW030435010526
44118CB00011B/650